VIETNAM DOC

An American Physician's Memoir

WILLIAM CLAYTON PETTY, MD

Retired, CAPT, USN, MC
Major, MC, US Army

Assigned: 24th Evacuation Hospital
Long Binh, Vietnam
October 1969 to Sept 1970

LifeRich PUBLISHING®

LifeRich Publishing is a registered trademark of The Reader's Digest Association, Inc.

LifeRich Publishing books may be ordered through booksellers or by contacting:

LifeRich Publishing
1663 Liberty Drive
Bloomington, IN 47403
www.liferichpublishing.com
1 (888) 238-8637

ISBN: 978-1-4897-0856-4 (sc)
ISBN: 978-1-4897-0857-1 (hc)
ISBN: 978-1-4897-0855-7 (e)

Library of Congress Control Number: 2016909607

Print information available on the last page.

LifeRich Publishing rev. date: 07/29/2016

CONTENTS

DEDICATION

T O ALL THE VETERANS OF the Vietnam War who were wounded and still struggle with disabilities. To the soldiers who died and to their loved ones who continue to struggle without them. To my wife, Zoe Leone, whom I love dearly and continues to struggle with me.

AUTHOR'S NOTE

THE CHARACTERS REFERRED TO IN this book are real. In some cases, I have used their real names but in others I have used pseudonyms to protect their privacy.

FOREWORD

FOR OVER FORTY YEARS I have tried to put the Vietnam War behind me and forget the incredible events I experienced. But I cannot. I still wake up with a fast pulse, rapid ventilation, and a feeling of imminent doom, after having repeated visions of wounded soldiers I cared for in Vietnam. On many occasions, Zoe Leone has comforted me until the uncontrollable sensations dissipate.

Memories of the Vietnam War are the most persistent, vivid memories of any period of my life. Memory experts tell us old memories can actually grow. The part of the memory that fades is the initial perception, the actual experience of the events. Every time we recall or reconstruct the memories, we have a tendency to add details from some succeeding event, making the initial event a little, or a lot, different than what really happened. I have certainly found this to be true of many memories not related to the Vietnam War. Details of my Vietnam war experience may not be as sharp as on the day of the event but the overall picture is accurate for certain events and impressions have been imbedded with resiliency. Those who shared the Vietnam War with me at the 24th Evacuation Hospital may tell a slightly different version of what happened. The difference will likely be one of perception or denial. We must remember when writing any history that the things of the past actually happened but history is only what someone wrote down.

This book was written in phases over forty-five years in various places: in Ohio, in Utah, in Ft. Lewis, Washington, and almost everywhere I spent time during those years. The final compilation was formalized in the summer of 2015.

Anesthesia is a gift from God to mankind. Administering anesthesia has been my privilege, my living, and my blessing. The Vietnam War was my baptism of fire in anesthesia for trauma. Wounded Soldiers in the Vietnam War were courageous, scared, deserving of good care, and a long way from home. I was determined to give my best to help the wounded to come home, a goal I know I accomplished. This book tells of my role in the Vietnam War. Laugh, cry, and share my feelings.

May the printed words on the pages of this book literally rise up to touch the innermost depths of your mind, stir you to think, and illuminate your thoughts to better understand the plight of wounded soldiers and the dedication of the doctors and nurses who care for them.

William Clayton Petty, M.D.
Anesthesiologist

CHAPTER 1

BEFORE VIETNAM

LIFE FOR ME BEGAN IN a rural town, Cedar City, in the mountains of Southern Utah. My mother said I was so small and frail at birth that she had to keep me in a cardboard box with a 100-watt bulb shining down on me to provide warmth (a homemade incubator!). Lots of young girls lived close by but there were only one or two boys in the neighborhood; so the neighborhood girls influenced my early years. Early sports consisted of playhouse, hopscotch, jacks, and roller skating, but eventually I advanced to football, basketball, and baseball [my favorite].

Kindergarten was great. For naps we slept on the floor on brown paper sheets but not before having milk and cookies from a loving teacher. First grade was initially a challenge. I did not do well and in an effort to improve my "scholarly adeptness" Miss Roberts moved me to the front row so I could "see" the blackboard. Miss Roberts told my mother I probably needed glasses so mom forthwith took me to the family physician where I gazed at the typical "E" eye chart. The doctor deduced with great intellect: Clayton does not know his alphabet; there is nothing wrong with his eyes. The truth is I could recite the alphabet frontwards and backwards! Thank God for persistent mothers! She made an appointment with the Ophthalmologist who came to Cedar City two or three times a year from Salt Lake City. He gave me the usual eye chart test and a few others and declared: Little wonder he could not see the blackboard; his eyesight is so bad that he will need glasses the rest of his life. Glasses opened up a new world for me. A world of blur opened into clarity and new perspectives. Now that I could see what was written on the blackboard, progress in school soared. However, the downside of wearing glasses was to suffer the vocal name-calling (e.g., nerd, four-eyes, smarty-pants) and the ridicule of those who did not have to wear glasses.

School is one thing I have loved intensely all my life. I have always been very curious and the challenge of learning has been a continual nourishment for my cerebrum. People who fail to spend the majority of waking hours learning about and contemplating the wonders of the earth and universe miss the real reason for living. Beginning in elementary school, through medical school, postgraduate training, and today, I have always had an intense drive to learn everything. How things work, the anatomy and physiology of plants and animals, where thoughts come from and what makes individual uniqueness, are a few of the wide range of subjects stimulating my intellect. If only I was intelligent enough to retain knowledge equal to my desire to learn.

In the early years of school and Boy Scouts I began to recognize how much the symbols of America meant to me. Class recital of the Pledge of Allegiance in school every day, placing a hand over the heart when the United States Flag goes by, standing up when the Star Spangled Banner is played, reverence for the Constitution of the United States, are just a few of the symbols still revered.

During one summer of World War II, my friends and I dug a hole in the backyard, covered it with boards and pretended we were soldiers in a foxhole. Of course, we were valiant soldiers fighting America's enemies: Hitler, Mussolini, and Tojo; names I knew little about except they killed our soldiers. In my mind America was always right, always the winner, and was without blemish. As a young man not old enough to vote, I participated enthusiastically in the political scene. In Junior High School I wanted Adali Stevenson to be elected President to the total dismay of my very Republican father. He and I had a lively diatribe centered on my Father's inability to see good in others and my stubbornness to accept negative comments about Democrats. Stevenson lost the election and I lost face at home, church, and school because of the strong dominance of Republicans in our community.

After graduating from high school I enrolled at our local college, the College of Southern Utah. I loved the challenge of University level classes and majored in biology and math. The College of Southern Utah was a land lease college so all male students were required to enroll in the Reserve Officers Training Corp [Air Force at the time]. In my senior year of high school, I had joined the Army Utah National Guard, so the military mode of thinking had already become a part of my life. The yearly two-week summer camp at Camp Williams, near Salt Lake City, was a highlight of the summer. Initially I served as the company clerk in the 222nd National Guard Unit, but later, after I learned how to use the slide rule more efficiently, I transferred to the artillery division. The military's high standards, discipline, comradeship, moral guidelines, and a love of country appealed to me.

After completing two years of college in Cedar City, I transferred to the University of Utah in Salt Lake City to finish pre-medical requirements for medical school. In 1958 candidates with a high scholastic record in the first three years of college were accepted into medical school without an interview or a bachelors degree. I was accepted after two and one-half years of undergraduate work to the University of Utah's medical school in early February 1959, with scheduled classes to begin in the fall.

In March 1959, I had a crisis of conscience. Was my religious faith true or a sham? My pragmatic thinking said: If the teachings of the Church of Jesus Christ of Latter-Day Saints is true then I should live them to the best of my ability, but if the teachings are not true then I should abandon the faith and follow the philosopher's precepts of moral living. I was encouraged by my roommates, all returned Mormon missionaries, to read the Book of Mormon, pray about it and find out for myself if the content came from God. I left my studies for about three days and read the Book of Mormon. After kneeling down beside my bed and asking to know if the book and source of the book was true, I came to have a testimony of its' truth. I decided I should not go to medical school but serve a mission for the Church of Jesus Christ of Latter Day Saints. I had previously turned down two requests by the Church to serve a mission prior to acceptance into medical school. After hours of deep thought, study, prayer, and counseling by one of the Church's Twelve Apostles, Elder LeGrande Richards, I decided I must serve a two-year mission for Christ. The Dean of the medical school was a non-Mormon and became very irate when I withdrew from the class of 1959. He told me in no uncertain terms I would never again be admitted to the University of Utah School of Medicine. I was heartbroken as I left his office but my religious convictions rang true. The Dean's secretary, Mrs. Florence Strong, told me not to worry because Deans come and go and I would be accepted again. She was right. One year later the Dean was replaced. My re-application, 18 months after withdrawing, was sent to the new Dean and I was accepted to medical school while still on my mission in Australia.

Serving a two year mission in Australia was an exciting adventure. As a missionary I served in Sydney, Brewarrina, Nyngan, Dubbo, The Entrance, and Maryborough. What a fantastic experience! Meeting people, exchanging ideas, learning a new culture, presenting the Gospel of Jesus Christ to others and seeing a few join the Church as they too acquired the same testimony of Christ I had. The people of Australia were wonderful and expressed gratitude for the "Yanks" saving Australia in World War II. It felt good hearing positive comments about the role of the United States military in Australia. Another building block of my patriotism.

Upon my return from the Australian mission in March 1961, I immediately enrolled in classes at the University of Utah. I had to complete the last quarter of undergraduate classes required for entrance into medical school, and worked hard all summer to save money for medical school in the fall. On the way home from Australia I arranged to spend three days in Hawaii to "court" Zoe Leone Palmer. Zoe Leone lived up the street from me during our growing up years and was now staying with her brother and his family in Hawaii. We had the same backgrounds, same morals, same religious convictions, and had dated a few times before I went to Australia. For three days we romanced in the soft enveloping warmth of the Hawaiian nights and decided to get married just one week before medical school started. We had a spiritual temple wedding, a fun but short honeymoon at the Grand Canyon, and then off to medical school.

During my third year of medical school I was accepted into the Army Senior Medical Student program. I received Second Lieutenant pay and privileges during the last nine months of medical school in exchange for an obligation to serve on active duty after my Army Internship. When medical school was completed we were off to Hawaii with our two children, Mason and Yvonne, to begin a rotating internship at Tripler Army Medical Center [TAMC].

Internship was like being chained to the hospital. Very little time off, an overwhelming workload, and long hours. Halfway through my internship, I contracted a respiratory virus, which I could not shake. I finally consulted a specialist in pulmonary care because I couldn't walk without coughing. The doctor wanted me to take few days off but I felt guilty making my fellow interns take my call and, of course, I remembered the small print on the bottom of the medical school certificate: *You are stoic, you cannot get sick, if you do get sick you must continue to work, you are invincible and can work 22 hours a day without making any mistakes, and the needs of the patients come before your needs.* I eventually cracked two ribs during a coughing episode and ended up as a patient in the respiratory care ward for ten days. The rotating internship provided an excellent exposure to various clinical specialties. During my rotation on anesthesia I decided the physiology and pharmacology aspects of anesthesia were just what I was looking for and I put my name in the pot for an anesthesiology residency.

At the beginning of my Internship in 1965, I had my first realistic exposure to the Vietnam War. In the early part of 1965 only a few soldiers were evacuated from Vietnam to TAMC. About four to five months after my arrival, the roof fell in as the Vietnam War became much hotter than military experts had predicted. In-country hospitals in Vietnam started filling up with casualties very fast. The military had to evacuate the wounded to out-of-country hospitals in Japan, the Philippines, and TAMC. Intern rotations on Orthopedics and Pulmonary medicine became nightmares. Nightfall on the orthopedic rotation usually meant meeting the buses filled with wounded soldiers arriving from Vietnam via Hickam Air Force Base. Medical work ups and admissions to the wards took all night and some patients' required immediate surgery. I remember vividly, one soldier who limped from the bus into the hospital. He still had his field uniform on, imbedded with sweat and covered with jungle dirt. His face emanated a look of disbelief. He ended up being my patient and I asked him why he looked so bewildered. He said he had gone to the field hospital in Vietnam with a sprained ankle and ended up being the "last patient to fill the beds." The next thing he knew he was on a jet plane headed to Hawaii. We X-rayed his ankle (no fracture), taped it up, got him some clean clothes, a shower, good food, a warm bed, and then sent him back to his unit in Vietnam three days later.

At the beginning of the internship, rotation on the pulmonary medicine ward was something every intern looked forward to. You had only one to four patients at a time during the three-month rotation; allowing time off in the afternoon to study or go to the beach. My time for rotation finally arrived and on my first day wounded soldiers from Vietnam came pouring in. During my three months on the pulmonary medicine ward every intern was assigned a minimum of thirty patients and sometimes as many as fifty.

Soldiers evacuated from Vietnam for infectious disease had maladies American doctors had only read about but never seen. No intern or resident had treated a patient with malaria, Denge fever, Tasahasihi fever, or any of the myriad of diseases from the jungle. But we soon learned how to diagnosis and treat these exotic tropical diseases. For instance, the diagnosis of malaria relapse required a blood smear to look for the parasite in the red blood cell. When the malaria parasite bursts the wall of the red blood cell, the residue of the red blood cell collects in the spleen. Sometimes such sequestration can overwhelm the spleen, cause it to rupture, requiring emergency surgery to save the soldier's life. Occasionally the hemoglobin from the red blood cells rupturing would be in such quantities the kidney would be obstructed, causing a syndrome called "black water fever", a sign usually indicative of ensuing death. When you were on call invariably someone would need a shot of Thorazine to relieve the lockjaw caused by the side effects of high dose anti-malarial drugs.

My heart went out to one particular soldier from upstate Maine recovering from malaria whose blood smears had been negative for three weeks and was on his way home the next day. In the early morning hours, he developed fever, chills, and a positive malaria smear, delaying his homecoming for another three weeks. He cried.

Many tropical diseases indigent to Vietnam were unknown even to our experienced staff physicians. Some of the diseases had not yet been described in the medical literature. I recall two nineteen-year old soldiers who arrived in excellent physical condition, except for a low fever, who rapidly developed fevers up to 108° F, and died within 24 hours, despite high doses of potent antibiotics. Autopsies failed to find the cause of death.

Following internship, I was assigned to Brooke Army Medical Center [BAMC] in San Antonio, Texas for a two residency in anesthesiology and a one-year fellowship in anesthesia research at Brooks School of Aerospace Medicine. My mentors basically fell into two categories: 1] seasoned military anesthesiologists and nurse anesthetists, and 2] young anesthesiologists who had been in academic settings and had pulled strings to get assigned to the "academic" program at BAMC. An excellent mix for a trainee: experience and wisdom from the seasoned military anesthesia providers and up to date science in anesthesia from the academic anesthesiologists. I learned practical anesthesia techniques from the seasoned anesthesia providers. One very important characteristic of how I practice anesthesia was learned from the Chief of the Anesthesia Service, Colonel Max Mendenhall. He could walk into a room in chaos during treatment for cardiac arrest, ask a few simple questions in a quiet, confident, voice, and get the cardiac arrest team calmed down and organized. It was an amazing scenario and took me three years to master the elements of how he did it. This one talent has served me well in anesthesia and flowed over into other fields of life.

Three years at BAMC provided a consistent exposure to soldiers from the Vietnam War. Vietnam veterans were having repeated plastic surgery procedures for extensive burns or other battle wounds. The burn unit at BAMC is world famous. Each week during the height of the Vietnam War, a United States Air Force (USAF) Florence Nightingale flight would fly from San Antonio to Vietnam to pick up burned soldiers, many were helicopter pilots, for transport and care at BAMC. Taking care of these soldiers, many with burns over 70% of their body, was not an easy or pleasant task.

The orthopedic service was always overflowing with Vietnam wounded. Beds with wounded soldiers lined all the walls of the wards and overflowed into the halls. Summertime in San Antonio is unbearable because of high humidity. Soldiers in casts were especially miserable. One day a Congressman visited the orthopedic wards, saw what misery the soldiers in casts were experiencing, and went back to Washington to arrange emergency funding for BAMC to install window air conditioning units.

One interesting but baffling syndrome of the amputees from the Vietnam War was "phantom limb." The soldier would be referred to the anesthesiologist with symptoms of intermittent severe pain or itching in the foot or hand of the limb blown off in Vietnam months ago. Not a usual phenomenon in amputees but seen frequently at BAMC. In 1966, treatment consisted of placing a needle at the anatomical level of the sympathetic nervous system corresponding to the symptoms and blocking the sympathetic nerves with a long acting local anesthetic. Invariably the soldier would get relief from the first one or two injections. If the relief lasted longer and longer after each injection, the soldier was then given a total of six injections, spaced one week apart. Sometimes the series of six injections stopped the symptoms, why? No one knows. If the soldier had relief from each injection for the same length of time [rare], they would be referred to the thoracic or general surgeon for a permanent surgical sympathectomy. Soldiers who got transient relief from only the first and/or second injections were not candidates for surgery or continuation of the series of six injections.

The neurosurgical ward at BAMC was packed to the brim with quadriplegics, paraplegics, and permanently brain damaged soldiers from the Vietnam War. Most were awaiting transfer to a Veterans Hospital nearest their home to receive whatever rehabilitation was available. Most of these injured soldiers were severely disabled for the remainder of their lives.

Each day I was in close contact with young soldiers struck down in the prime of life by the ravages of war. These soldiers were not only suffering physical pain but were also suffering from the mental anguish of rejection by family members and certain citizens of the United States. One thing was positive in their lives, they were receiving moral support, love, and understanding from the medical and nursing staff at BAMC.

As the end of my third year of anesthesiology training approached I was placed on orders for Vietnam. In preparation for the Vietnam War assignment the army sent physicians to the Vietnam War Orientation at Camp Bullis, near San Antonio. The only thing interesting about Camp Bullis was the numerous blinds built in the trees for the annual dear hunt in Texas. We spent a couple of days crawling under barbed wire with machine guns firing over our heads, firing a pistol, the M-16 rifle, and listening to Vietnam Veterans tell us about how to act if you became a prisoner of war. My time in orientation was very limited because the army needed my warm body to take care of soldiers at the hospital. The Army was short-handed for physicians and especially anesthesiologists throughout the Vietnam War. For this reason, I was never assigned to the six week "charm school" for drafted physicians held at Fort Sam Houston. I was scheduled to go to the course immediately after medical school, then again after my internship, and again just before shipping out to Vietnam. Each time my orders were canceled for the "good of the Army." Because I missed the "charm school", I never learned officially how to salute, march, or show proper respect for senior officers. I already had acquired these skills from my service in the Utah National Guard.

Resident training at BAMC was an experience I will always cherish. Yes, we worked long hours, but the immense variety of patients and diseases was an excellent training experience. Residents had a tremendous load of responsibility. The anesthesia didactic program at BAMC was well planned and linked to the Air Force anesthesia program at Wilford Hall Hospital and the University of Texas anesthesia program in San Antonio. During the last six months of my senior year I served as senior resident. This position afforded me the opportunity to learn and apply leadership skills under the close supervision of staff anesthesiologists. On arrival in Vietnam, I was ready [even thought I didn't think so at the time] to take care of the many mutilated soldiers and the responsibilities of the Chief of Anesthesia.

Our family, Mason, Yvonne, Kendall, and Valerie, spent the month of September, 1969, in Cedar City, Utah finding a place for them to live while I was in Vietnam. God blessed us with a small rental house on the same street as Zoe Leone's parents, her uncle, and two aunts. I knew when I left for the Vietnam War on Thursday, 9 October 1969 at 1043hrs, that my wife and family were in good hands. Before I left Cedar City I arranged for flowers to be sent to Zoe Leone, my mother, and my mother-in-law. I also went to the Iron County Record, and paid $10.00 for an advertisement to be published in the issue closest to Christmas, wishing the family Merry Christmas. I wanted to include the advertisement in the photo section but the Iron Country Record went out of business and the copyright permission was impossible to trace.

Official Orders For Vietnam

DEPARTMENT OF THE ARMY
HEADQUARTERS 44TH MEDICAL BRIGADE
APO SAN FRANCISCO 96384

SPECIAL ORDERS*   EXTRACT   14 OCTOBER 1969
NUMBER 267

66.TC 254. RSG dir as indic this sta. NTI.

PETTY, WILLIAM C 0529480381 MAJ MC 3115 HHD 68TH Med
    GP WBHEAAA APO SF 96491
Asg TO: 24th Evac Hosp WBHEAAA APO SF 96491
PCM(MDC): N200
Auth: VOCO 68th Med Gp   Rept date: 13 Oct 69
ADC: NA Comp: NA   BASO:NA   DEROS:8Oct 70 EDCSA:20Oct69
Sp. instr: MA

FOR THE COMMANDER:

OFFICIAL: JAMES H. LINDAHL
               CPT, MSC
               Adjutant

JOHN H. WILLIAMS
CW2, USA
Asst Adjutant

DISTRIBUTION:
5- Indiv conc
1-CG USARV   ATTN:AVHSUL-P APO SF 96375
15 - Consol orders   1-Rec file
1-222d PSC Data Proc Br APO SF 96491
10-CP HHD 68th Med Gp APO SF 96491
5-CO 36th Evac Hosp APO SF 96491
10-CO 24th Evac Hosp APO SF 96491
5-CO 345th Med Det APO SF 96291
5-CO 93d Evac Hosp APO SF 96491
35-222d PSC Team A APO SF 96491
15-222d PSC Team A ATTN:MR APO SF 96491

*Retyped from original orders. Names of other soldiers going to Vietnam were
omitted.

CHAPTER 2

THE 24TH EVACUATION HOSPITAL

T HE 24TH EVACUATION HOSPITAL, OPENED in July 1966, was the largest military hospital in the southern half of South Vietnam. A 300-bed multi-specialty hospital fully staffed for general, thoracic, neurological, orthopedic, maxillofacial [oral surgery, plastic, and ENT], urological, cardiovascular, obstetrical/gynecological, and ophthalmological surgery. During the period November 1969 to September 1970, the hospital averaged 953 admissions and 385 major operations per month. At any given time 16 to 25 percent of the wounded soldiers were listed as seriously ill or very seriously ill, and an average of nine were on ventilators. The average stay in the hospital before evacuation to Japan was six to eight days, with a range of one to 62 days.

The 24th Evacuation Hospital was located on Long Binh Army Post, a military complex twenty-five miles square, sixteen miles from Saigon and housing the headquarters of the United States Army Vietnam (USARV). Long Binh Army Post was home for over 50,000 soldiers and cost approximately $100 million to build. The hospital's location within the post boundaries was relatively safe; far enough away from the gasoline storage area and a good distance from the most sought after target of the Viet Cong on post, the ammunition dump. The Viet Cong frequently attempted to blow up the ammunition dump by launching mortars from outside the fence, or by sending sappers [Viet Cong dressed in black] under the barbed wire to set explosives. When the ammo dump was successfully hit there was literally a fourth of July fireworks display. I do recall one tragedy not far from the site of the 24th Evacuation Hospital. A small medical clinic received a mortar shell in mid-day and a physician was killed, the only physician casualty I knew of during the war.

The 24th Evacuation Hospital was the surgical specialty referral hospital for the southern half of South Vietnam. The majority of wounded soldiers were examined in the field by a medic, stabilized for evacuation and arrived from the site of injury, usually by helicopter, within 30 minutes. Most of the wounded soldiers were frightened and worried but maintained an outward composure of calm. I do not recall any injured soldier with hysteria similar to that I have witnessed in some severely traumatized patients in the U.S. Perhaps the difference in reaction to trauma is the training and comradeship of the soldiers coupled with the lifting of fear of being taken out of the jungle. At the 24th Evacuation Hospital the wounded soldier felt safe, he was getting medical care, and, most likely, on his way home. Good medical care was a major morale booster for soldiers in the jungle. Soldiers knew if they were wounded they would be evacuated to medical care at all costs. They also knew if they arrived at a hospital alive they had a very good chance of going home. The statistics of survival from massive injury in Vietnam has never been surpassed in any other war or in any civilian trauma program in the world. The 24th Evacuation Hospital had a 2-3% mortality rate, which meant if you arrived alive at the 24th you had a 98% change of leaving the hospital alive. An amazing statistic! Many soldiers with multiple injuries would not have survived if treated in the majority of trauma centers in the U. S. today. I take great pride in being part of a team that provided the finest trauma care in the history of the world. A record that will stand for a long time.

The 24th Evacuation hospital was near the U.S. Military Jail, the Army Tropical Disease center, and a small Army exchange [PX]. The hospital had been constructed from Quonset huts laid out in rectangular formation. Next to the patient receiving area was a large helicopter landing pad. One section of the hospital was isolated from the main structure, was surrounded by barbed wire, and served as the Prisoner of War hospital. The Walter Reed Army Institute of Research [WRAIR] from Washington, D.C., had a small wing. WRAIR studied the physiological aspects of trauma and tried to develop better ways to treat trauma. The WRAIR unit provided us with the only blood gas machine available for miles. Arterial blood samples from the operating room and Intensive Care Units [ICUs] let us know the status of the oxygen, carbon dioxide, and acid-base balance of a soldier's blood. In 1969, routine analysis of arterial blood was not common and to have such a modality available in Vietnam was a plus for soldier care. Another spinoff from WRAIR was the opportunity to participate in clinical research projects.

The helicopter-landing pad was the heart of operations. The dedication and bravery of the helicopter pilots was, in great part, responsible for our 98% success rate. Just like "Mash," the sound of rotating helicopter blades meant it was time to go to work. Helicopters were constantly flying over the hospital but you learned to recognize characteristic changes in rotor blade rotation prior to landing on our pad. Today, every time I hear a helicopter, my mind, for a split second, takes me back to Vietnam and I mentally prepare to go to work. My experience with helicopters makes it easy for me to sympathize with soldiers who were exposed to gun fire in the jungle and today hit the dirt when they hear the backfire of a car or a firecracker exploding. These reactions are imbedded for the rest of your life.

On arrival in Vietnam I made it a point to inspect the building where the compressed medical gas cylinders [e.g. oxygen and nitrous oxide] were stored. Storage conditions were within the recommendations of the Compressed Gas Association of the U.S. except for my discovery of cylinders of cyclopropane. Cyclopropane is an inhalation anesthetic stored under pressure in a cylinder. Cyclopropane, often referred to as the "champagne" of anesthesia in it's heyday, was an excellent anesthetic but by 1969 the drug was rarely used in the U.S. For some reason, cyclopropane had found a niche in the Army supply system and cylinders of the gas were sitting in a storage shed on the edge of the helicopter pad. I calmly explained to the Sergeant in charge that cyclopropane was explosive and if the cylinders got hot or fell over, the hut he was standing in and any helicopter on the pad would immediately be engulfed in flames. With a wild look in his eyes, he asked me what to do. I instructed him to take the cylinders to a far away place and bury them. Our anesthesia machines were built to administer cyclopropane but we would not be using cyclopropane on my watch. He looked relieved; I know I was!

Multiple Quonset huts were arranged in rows around a central rectangular lawn. One end of each ward, the operating room, the intensive care units, and the receiving hut surrounded this central open lawn where soldiers and sometimes staff would congregate at night. Included in the hospital compound was a mess hall, supply office, Office of the Commander, personnel section, Red Cross Volunteer's office, and a small vendor truck selling hot dogs and soft drinks. Many nights the central lawn area was filled with the strong scent of grass burning [marijuana]. The female nurse's quarters were a large fenced in building adjacent to the hospital wards. About ninety degrees on the other side of the hospital were quarters for male officers and male enlisted personnel. Adjacent to the officer's quarters was a large shower stall and latrine. On top of the showers was a water tank with a heater that provided intermittent heavenly hot showers. Walking wooden platforms [two by fours with wood slats between them] connected the personnel living quarters with the hospital. The wooden platforms were especially useful in keeping us out of the mud during the tremendous downpours of the rainy season.

Army and civilian cooks staffed the mess hall. A large ceiling fan made it bearable to eat in the mess hall. Food was great. Fresh vegetables were flown into Long Binh from military farms in Thailand. Occasionally ice cream would be featured on the menu. Grunts from the jungle were especially appreciative of the "hot food." During the night when we were working, someone from the mess hall would bring huge plates of sandwiches accompanied by cold milk and other snacks. The mess hall personnel were always supportive of our long working hours during mass casualties. Extended work hours left little time for regular exercise so my waist line would have grown two or three inches if I had eaten at the mess hall on a regular basis. Alternate eating sites consisted of the vendor truck, cans of sardines or Vienna sausages purchased at the PX, or cooking in our hooch "backyard." Every hooch had a fifty-gallon drum cut in half on a stand with a wire grill on top. Charcoal was easily obtained and the mess hall would provide the food to cook.

At Christmas there was a lull in fighting and the Chaplains arranged for the children in a nearby orphanage to visit us for the day. The mess hall was the center of activity. Roast turkey and all the trimmings, topped off with ice cream for dessert. Members of the hospital staff, enlisted and officers, volunteered to participate and were assigned two children to be with during dinner and for the visit of Santa Claus. My two assigned children did not speak any English but the love exchanged through our eyes, laughter, hugs, and smiles made up for any oral communication. A lovely day of memories despite the fact I cried because I was not at home with Zoe Leone and the children.

Humidity was very high in Long Binh. A freshly laundered uniform would be soaked after walking 50 yards to the hospital. By 1969 the 24th Evacuation Hospital had window air conditioning units in the operating rooms, the receiving area, and the wards. During the era prior to air conditioning, wounded soldiers were given large volumes of intravenous fluids during surgery to replace the excessive fluid loss from exposed intestines, etc. Without air conditioning all operating personnel would literally wring water out of their surgical attire after each case. Air conditioning was a blessing and many nights when my air conditioner was on the blink I would go to my small office in the operating room to write letters or read.

Wounded soldiers arrived by helicopters day and night. Rarely did a soldier come by ground ambulance. Wounded soldiers were taken to the receiving area on the same stretchers used in flight. A team of highly trained doctors and enlisted men and women examined each soldier and began the resuscitative process. Intravenous lines were started, oxygen was given through nasal prongs, clothes were removed with scissors, blood was washed off to expose the wound, samples of blood were taken for the laboratory and blood bank, and an immediate evaluation was made of the surgical status of the soldier. Each shift was supervised by a triage surgeon responsible for determining the order of surgery for all arrivals. He based his triage on experience and an unwritten priority list: American soldiers first, Allied soldiers second, POWs third, and civilians last. Two other priority lists existed, 1] critically wounded and 2] those who could wait until after the critically wounded had been cared for. For example, if a critically wounded Thailand soldier arrived just after an American soldier with a broken leg, the Thai soldier would go first and the American soldier would wait for an open operating room. Critically wounded soldiers in need of immediate surgery were scheduled for the next operating room. Soldiers needing surgery of a less than critical nature, e.g. broken arm, might be sent to X-ray before returning to the holding area to await surgery. We worked until every American soldier, Allied soldier, enemy soldier, and civilian was taken care of. When no casualties were waiting, the operating room was shut down, cleaned, and restocked. As soon as a casualty requiring surgery arrived, the operating room was reopened, any time, day or night. This proved to be a very efficient system to take care of the wounded.

Operating rooms in the battlefield were not the same as in the United States. The operating room Quonset hut was divided in half by a permanent partition, and then each half was further divided by "move-around" wooden partitions. The area between two moveable partitions was called a "room". Usually four rooms were occupied when we were receiving casualties and sometimes all eight of the rooms were opened. Concrete floors were hosed down with water and mopped between cases. Personnel wore combat boots because the floor was usually covered with water and blood. Oxygen for the operating rooms was supplied in large compressed cylinders of "H" size (51 inches high). The oxygen cylinders were under a pressure of 2000 psig, the nitrous oxide cylinders under a pressure of 750 psig, and both were considered dangerous. Usually the cylinders were secured in the upright position by chains attached to the wall behind the anesthesia machine.

Electrical sockets in the entire facility were at risk because civilian contract "electricians" were either drunk or did not know what they were doing when they installed the electrical outlets. "Qualified" contract electricians from outside Vietnam were responsible for installing and maintaining the electrical systems in United States buildings throughout Vietnam. What I saw and experienced with the electrical system in the 24th Evacuation Hospital was a sham: poorly done, very expensive, and a threat to our patients. One episode caused by the defective electrical system illustrates my point:

> One afternoon a soldier for a neurosurgical operation in the prone position had his spinal canal open from the neck to the hip. We were filling the canal with ice in an attempt to keep the spinal cord from further swelling and causing post spinal shock syndrome. One of the ECG machines became available late in the case and it was decided to hook it up to this soldier

for monitoring. The leads were placed on the soldier first. When the ECG machine was plugged into the electrical socket the soldier was literally lifted off the table like he had been shocked with a defibrillator. The ECG was immediately unplugged. Since the soldier had received an unknown amount of electrical current, we had to immediately cover the wound, turn him over, and give him closed chest massage until his heart started again. He recovered from the electrical shock but his combat spinal injury left him paraplegic. Did the adverse electrical event change the course of his recovery? No one knows the answer.

This case is illustrative of the kind of equipment problems faced on a daily basis. Electrical connections could never be relied on. Other problems occurred but were not as dramatic as the case presented.

A short distance from the hospital was a prison facility for American soldiers. Soldiers in the jail had been involved in violent acts and some soldiers were psychotic, sadistic, and considered very dangerous. The soldiers were being kept in the jail until they could be transferred to the United States for court martial and then transfer to a federal penitentiary. The Commander of the jail occasionally came to our hooch for dinner. He related how dangerous the prisoners were and how security had to be very tight in order to keep the prisoners from killing the prison guards. One night the base power went off. A young officer on duty immediately called an armored battalion, including tanks, to surround the jail. Portable lights were placed around the perimeter to light up the jail. Blaring megaphones woke us up. The rapid action of the young officer was deemed to have saved lives. Occasionally a prisoner came to the hospital for treatment and my impression was these prisoner soldiers appeared much more dangerous than the prisoners from the Utah State Prison I later saw at the University of Utah.

My Hooch

Quonset huts had been partitioned into individual rooms. My rank of Major rated me a small one-man room, but I lucked out and was assigned a room with one-half of an old in-window air conditioner. Someone had cut a hole in the wall of the Quonset hut and mounted an air conditioner that blew air into my room and the room next door. A civilian worker had apparently been "bribed" with a few bottles of whiskey to install the air conditioner. The air conditioner had been purchased and installed prior to my tour of duty so I was obligated to pay $100 to the previous occupant. When I left I received a similar amount from the next person assigned to the room. It is impossible to describe what a blessing the air conditioner was on a hot humid day after working continuously for 48 hours.

My room was about 7 feet by 8 feet. I was able to build a bed frame, a headboard, and a closet. Lumber was obtained from medical supply shipping crates and tools from the hospital carpentry kit. Good luck intervened and I was able to buy a small refrigerator at the local PX. Personal refrigerators were a hot item and did not last long once delivered and put on sale. I happened to walk into the PX just as a new shipment was being put on the shelf. Now I had a place to keep soda pop, cans of Vienna sausages, and other little items, thus making life a bit more pleasant. A de-humidifier rod inside the closet kept my clothes from rotting and limited fungal growth in my boots. Papers were kept dry if placed on the top shelf of the closet. At the head of the bed I built a small shelf for a stereo and earphones. Electrical outlets were in every room and no one ever received a monthly electrical bill!

Orders for personal goods were sent directly to the "Vietnam War" Sears warehouse on the West Coast for purchase of wallpaper, curtains, mattresses, blankets, lights, or just about anything you could think of. Depth of choice in the very small PX was limited and the PX was not air conditioned, hot, and always crowded. About all that was stocked in any quantity were soda pop, cigarettes, snacks, and writing paper. Occasionally a shipment of electronic goods arrived and was always sold out in a few hours. The military PX system in Japan supplied a mail order catalog and orders for china, crystal, stereos, silverware, etc., could be sent either to Vietnam or directly to the U.S.

On arrival in Vietnam you were required to exchange U.S. dollars for Military Payment Certificates (MPC). By limiting the amount of U.S. currency in circulation the military hoped to suppress the number of greenbacks falling into the hands of the Viet Cong. The MPC script system ended up being a failure; costing the American public many tax dollars. Black market dollars were collected, packaged, and sent to North Vietnam for purchasing military weapons and supplies. MPC could be used anywhere, including restaurants in Saigon. Upon departure from Vietnam, MPC was exchanged for greenbacks at the exiting air terminal.

Each Quonset hut was surrounded by a protective wall of sandbags stacked about four feet high. By 1969 the original sandbags were deteriorating and spewing sand. About twenty yards from my hooch was the officer latrine and shower. In the night if I had to urinate, I just stepped outside the hut and let go. I appeared in front of the Hospital Commander on a couple of occasions and was sternly warned I would be given an Article 15 if I did not stop my nocturnal practices. For community health reasons the Commander was probably right but convenience was certainly served by the "short trip".

The showers near the officer's quarters were a godsend. When you were tired and covered with blood and sweat, it was wonderful to just stand under the shower with the hot water running. What a spectacular moment!

Chronic fatigue made sleeping easy. Sometimes the party noises in adjoining hooch's would wake you and these parties had a tendency to start any time, night or day. But noise was not the only thing that could wake you up. One night I was awakened by something crawling on my face. I grabbed it, threw it hard against the wall, and went back to sleep. When I awoke the next morning the critter on my cheek had been a four-inch cockroach. It was not uncommon to have large insects and other wonderful pests, i.e. large rats, interrupt sleep.

Our beds were made every day by the Mamasons [Vietnamese female civilians] hired collectively by everyone in the hooch. Each hooch occupant paid about $40.00 a month for two Mamasons to launder clothes, shine boots, make beds, clean rooms, and keep the general area of the hooch in order. Mamasons were not overwhelmed with work because we spent most of our time in the hospital and did not get our rooms very untidy. When the Mamasons were having lunch, cooking smells could be detected at least 50 feet away. Their food was always flavored with a sauce call ncocmon. Ncocmon was an all-purpose, very salty, smelly, sauce made from decayed fish. Fish were placed in a fifty-gallon drum and allowed to rot. After three to six months the solids from the fish, i.e. bones, settled to the bottom and the top layer of liquid, the ncocmon, was spooned into jars. Food prepared by the Mamasons was certainly a taste treat, but I cannot say I would want it on a daily basis.

When I was not working I spent most of the time sleeping, resting, or listening to music. Rarely was I awake and alert enough to study for my upcoming exams for Board Certification in Anesthesiology. I had finished a two-year residency in anesthesiology and a year of anesthesia research training just before my assignment to Vietnam. Anesthesia Board Certification was divided into two sections: a written examination and, one year later, an oral examination. I had successfully passed the written examination prior to Vietnam and during my tour in Vietnam I had to "bone up" for the oral examination. I knew I was getting enough clinical exposure but the didactic portion was a bit lacking. I passed the oral examination with great trepidation shortly after my tour of duty in Vietnam.

Many nights, after working with wounded soldiers all day, brought reflection on how fortunate and blessed I was to be living in such wonderful circumstances at the 24th Evacuation Hospital. Soldiers in the jungle were being bitten by insects, exposed to exotic diseases and facing death daily. Tired and worn down as I was, I could never complain that my situation was as bad as the soldiers who constantly put their life in harms way. It was always an honor and privilege for me to serve the wounded soldiers.

Supply

Adequate hospital supplies were absolutely vital to the quest for excellent medical care. Through the doors of the hospital's supply warehouse came the intravenous fluids, medications, anesthetics, surgical instruments, blood administration sets and filters, dressings, tape, syringes, needles, spinal sets, cylinders of oxygen and nitrous oxide, and a multitude of other essential medical supplies. When ordering supplies in-country it was essential to be very careful with the words on the order form. Once I ordered twelve individual sets of disposable spinal trays for spinal anesthesia. Somehow the order left the hospital requesting twelve cases. Three months later when the spinal trays arrived, the supply Sergeant called and asked where to store the cases of spinal trays about to be off loaded. Imagine my surprise to be looking at 144 sets of disposable spinal trays, enough to last our hospital for at least ten years. Solution: take the twelve disposable spinal trays we needed and send the remaining 132 trays to the Vietnamese Army Hospital in Saigon. The excess trays could not be returned and the U.S. Military did not need extra spinal trays in-country. Better to "support" the allies than let an essential medical commodity go to waste.

Basically four methods were used to obtain medical supplies: 1] direct pick up at the main supply depot on Long Binh, 2] order the item and wait three months for delivery, 3] get authorization from the Military Assistance Command Vietnam (MACV) Surgeon to order the item on a 24-hour emergency delivery to Vietnam from the U.S., or, and always our last choice, 4] get the item from the black market in Saigon. In the early part of the war, when involvement of the U.S. in the Vietnam War began escalating, massive supplies were stock piled in Vietnam. Supply depots were originally stocked from "emergency" depots in the U.S. designed to be sent anywhere in the world. As a result, the main supply depot for Long Binh had jungle oriented supplies, as well as, skies, parkas, and desert equipment.

The 24th Evacuation Hospital did not have any electrocardiograms [ECG] when I arrived, so I visited the main supply depot on Long Bing one afternoon in an attempt to find some. The supply Sergeant tried to find ECG in the supply card file but was unsuccessful. He told me to go out back and if I could find an ECG in a crate it was mine. I walked through the door and found myself looking at about ten acres of boxes and containers! To my surprise, after only two hours of searching, I stumbled upon three crates labeled ECG. When opened they each contained a state-of-the-art ECG. All three crates were loaded on the back of the jeep, unpacked at the 24th Evacuation Hospital, and used continually until the hospital was shut down years later. The two-hour search was educational and productive to say the least.

The delivery time for the great majority of medical supplies was three months. Loading, transporting, and unloading supplies from ships was tedious. Consistently used items, i.e. intravenous fluids, were on standing orders but items like spinal trays and tracheostomy tubes were ordered as needed and sometimes it was difficult to predict exactly how many to keep on hand. Storage area was limited in the hospital and there was very little room for items requiring refrigeration.

When a critical item, e.g. tracheostomy tube, was depleted and needed immediate replacement, the 24-hour emergency system was instituted. To my knowledge, no one abused the system because everyone recognized how vital it was to the welfare of soldiers. A physician at the hospital initiated the order, the supply Sergeant typed it up, and the Chief of Surgery or Commander of the hospital called the Military Assistant Command Vietnam [MACV] Surgeon to request the item[s] stating the justification for the extreme need. The MACV Surgeon authorized the buy and turned the request over to the in-country purchasing agent. A telephone call was made directly to the manufacturer of the item[s] in the U.S., a purchase order number was given for payment, and arrangements were made for the manufacturer to take the item[s] to the nearest airport or for the military to pick it up and take it to the nearest airport, where it was flown to the West Coast to be put on the next airplane [troop carrier or provisions] destined for Vietnam. When the item(s) arrived in Vietnam, a helicopter flew them immediately to the 24th Evacuation Hospital. The 24-hour system saved many lives.

The least used method of supply acquisition was the Saigon black market. It was rumored the dockworkers in Saigon were "allowed" to steal up to 15% of the ship's cargo when off-loading cargo ships. A cache of black market merchandise was displayed on blankets laid on the ground in certain streets in Saigon. All kinds of surgical instruments were available. The choice of surgical instruments on the black market was usually superior to our own and we were one of the best-supplied American military hospitals in Vietnam. One experience, close to home, made a major impression on how effective and efficient the black market supply system worked. A 2 1/2-ton Army truck was loaded with wool blankets at the main supply depot on Long Binh, destined for the 24th Evacuation Hospital. The truck did not stop en-route, but when it arrived all the blankets were missing!

In November 1972 the 24th Evacuation Hospital, after a history of excellent care to soldiers, was transferred to the South Vietnamese Army.

CHAPTER 3

ANESTHESIA

T HE REASON I WAS ORDERED to Vietnam was to administer anesthesia to soldiers wounded in combat. All anesthesia support personnel and equipment were in Vietnam for one purpose: administration of safe anesthesia.

An anesthesia machine is required to administer general anesthesia safely. During the Vietnam War the U.S. Armed Services provided a rugged versatile anesthesia machine, the *Military Field Anesthesia Machine, Model 785*. The components of the machine were adequate to meet the needs of combat anesthesia. The entire machine fit into one metal carrying case, weighing about 85 pounds. The carrying case separated into two equal parts once the holding straps were released. One half of the case contained the guts of the machine and the other half of the case held the accessories necessary to make the machine functional [reducing valves, hoses, etc.]. It took about thirty minutes to get the machine operational. Re-packaging the machine for transport required about one hour; each piece had to fit "just right" in order to close and lock the two-piece case. The Model 785 anesthesia machine was capable of delivering the following anesthetic gases: oxygen, nitrous oxide, cyclopropane, and ether. By the time of the Vietnam War, cyclopropane and ether were rarely used in the United States because both agents were a fire hazard and were not as safe as other anesthetics readily available at the time, e.g. halothane. However, no contingency had been made for the safe administration of halothane by the Model 785 anesthesia machine. To use halothane required a "Rube Goldberg" fitting to allow anesthetic gases to flow through a halothane vaporizer. After the Vietnam War, the Model 785 anesthesia machine was replaced by the Model 885 which had a "Universal" vaporizer capable of safely administering all liquid anesthetics, i.e. ether, halothane, forane, etc. History, thus far, has shown that the development of military anesthesia machines to meet the needs of anesthesia providers is always just one war behind.

Once the Model 785 anesthesia machine was assembled and tested, it was positioned at the head of the operating room table. Each machine received maximal use during the Vietnam War. I can safely vouch that the Model 785 was a very dependable anesthesia machine requiring minimal maintenance. An essential add-on to the anesthesia machine was a Bird® ventilator. A ventilator was essential in order to have both hands free for blood administration as soon as the endotracheal tube was placed and the initial ventilator settings initiated. The Bird® ventilator was a component of anesthesia services specified in the Army supply depot and, fortunately, was easy to repair. The main drawback of the Bird® Ventilator was the need for repeated adjusting of the ventilator settings to meet the needs of the constant changes in lung compliance. The Bird® ventilator was a pressure dependent ventilator, e.g. it delivered gases until a preset pressure was reached, as opposed to a volume dependent ventilator that delivers the same volume over a wide range of pressures. Lung injuries and massive blood transfusions were usually associated with wide swings in lung compliance, therefore, the pressure settings on the Bird® ventilator had to be reset frequently.

The anesthesia machine and the ventilator required compressed medical gases for operation. Large cylinders of oxygen [H-tanks] were stored in the upright position against the wall of the operating room. During a mass casualty the operating rooms would run continuously for 48 hours or longer. Oxygen supply was paramount to support anesthesia and the large oxygen cylinders had to be changed frequently. Handling multiple, heavy, bulky oxygen cylinders necessitated a certain risk under the best of conditions. Operating rooms at the 24th Evacuation Hospital would certainly not be described as "...the best of conditions." I recall one incident when a full oxygen cylinder fell off a transport cart in the operating room. The fall jarred loose the control valve on the top of the cylinder, a potentially devastating event. Each oxygen cylinder is built to hold oxygen compressed at about 2000 pounds per square inch [psig] [atmospheric pressure surrounding us is only 14 pounds per square inch]. Releasing 2000 psig of oxygen all at once, e.g. when the cylinder valve breaks completely off, can cause the cylinder to fly through the air like a torpedo. Such an airborne cylinder is capable of going through a three-foot thick cement wall. We were lucky the cylinder valve stem did not break off, only the control on the cylinder valve was opened. Oxygen escaped at hurricane force. Debris on the cement floors boiled like a desert dust storm and immediately engulfed eight operating room spaces. Surgeons and nurses covered the soldier's open wounds with sterile sheets to prevent contamination. Fortunately, one brave young soldier straddled the gushing cylinder on the floor and closed the cylinder valve. An exciting time to say the least!

Each anesthesia provider kept an anesthesia cart stocked with the drugs, equipment, and gadgets required to keep the soldier safely asleep and administer massive transfusions. In the United States such carts are similar to auto mechanics carts, with many different sized pull out drawers and a nice level top to work on. In Vietnam, anesthesia providers made carts by building on the framework of a small stainless steel table usually used for in-surgery purposes. The tables came with only with one pull out drawer. Each anesthesia provider designed their cart to best fit their style of administration of anesthesia. Usually cardboard cubby holes held together with two or three-inch adhesive tape were attached to the main frame of the stainless steel cart. These cubby holes held the airways, endotracheal tubes, intravenous catheters, blood pumps, blood transfusion sets, and a host of other essential items. Cardboard drawer dividers made it easy to access the anesthesia drugs, i.e. atropine, lidocaine, pentothal, steroids, etc.

Two portable suction apparatus were positioned at the head of the table during the induction of anesthesia in case the soldier vomited voluminous quantities of processed food or previously swallowed blood. Monitoring was simplistic compared to today's array of technology. Every soldier had a manual blood pressure cuff on the arm or leg, and either a chest or esophageal stethoscope. There were only three Electrocardiogram machines available for eight operating rooms.

Every soldier had a minimum of two intravenous lines started with the highest diameter catheter available. The diameter of a catheter is defined by its gauge [ga] number, e.g. 10ga, 12ga, 14ga, 16ga,18ga, 20g. The smaller the number, i.e. 12ga, the larger the diameter of the catheter; the larger the diameter of the catheter the greater the volume of blood can be delivered per minute. Almost all wounded soldiers had a 14ga catheter and many had two or more 12ga catheters. Giving thirty units of whole blood in one hour through large diameter catheters was a task quickly mastered by anesthesia providers.

Soldiers were carried to the operating room on the same stretcher used for helicopter transport. These simple stretchers similar to those depicted in World War I, World War II, and Korean War movies; two poles on each side of a piece of reinforced canvas. Wooden rectangular platforms in the triage area held the stretchers at the appropriate level to provide care to the soldier. The hospital accumulated stashes of stretchers but eventually the stretchers were rotated back to the evacuation helicopters and ambulances.

Before putting the soldier to sleep the anesthesia provider always made an attempt to talk to the soldier. Communication was very important to allay fears associated with being wounded, being alone far from home, being separated from "war buddies," and facing pending surgery. Most wounded soldiers welcomed with open arms the temporary pain relief and separation from the "real world" provided by the anesthetic. Most soldiers had genuine concerns about what was happening, what was going to be done, i.e. amputation of the leg vs. repair of a blood vessel to save the leg, and would they be sent back to the field. Others were comatose or so critically injured that a meaningful discussion was futile.

Many soldiers sustained multiple injuries. The associated massive blood loss caused severe hypotension, rapid heart rate, and, sometimes, hypoxemia. Most of the injured soldiers were young and in good health which were important factors for surviving injuries that would have caused death in older patients with associated diseases in the United States. I recall more than one soldier who could still talk coherently with a blood pressure so low the blood pressure cuff could not detect it and no palpable pulses at the wrist and femoral arteries. The only pulse present was the carotid artery in the neck. These particular soldiers had basically shut down all blood supply to non-critical areas, i.e. legs and arms, and were shunting all the oxygenated blood to the brain and heart to maintain life.

Soldiers awake but without detectable blood pressure and those comatose were not given a general anesthetic during the first part of surgery. Instead, we would give them 100% oxygen to breathe, a muscle relaxant drug to paralyze all skeletal muscles, rapidly place an endotracheal tube into the trachea, start the ventilator, and then furiously work on replacing the massive blood loss. The surgeons would open the abdomen and/or chest and tie off all the bleeding blood vessels, helping us to fill the circulation without blood leaking out of open-ended vessels. Once the soldier's blood pressure was detectable and the heart rate slowed, a pain killer, like Demerol or Fentanyl, could be safely introduced. As physiological conditions continued to improve, a little nitrous oxide (a general anesthetic) and eventually a potent anesthetic like halothane were introduced. Every time a drug was added the soldier's vital signs were carefully monitored to make sure they were tolerating the new drug. The entire anesthetic was carefully formulated to make sure the soldier was safe and had the best chance for survival.

During every case in which general anesthetic could not be induced from the start, it was absolutely vital to stay in verbal contact with the soldier, even when you had no idea if they could comprehend what was being said. You told them they were paralyzed while awake in order to do surgery to save their life. You carefully assured them that at as soon as possible you would give drugs to stop the terrible pain and fright they were suffering. A continuous one-way dialog with the soldier throughout the procedure was vital because you did not know the full extent of blood circulation and, therefore, could not ascertain the effect of administered drugs. Many of the soldiers did recall events and conversations during the operation. When making ward rounds the next day I always asked the soldiers if they remembered anything and/or if they recalled any pain. Many recalled conversations, some recalled both conversations and pain, but **not one** soldier complained of the ordeal. Invariably, the soldier would express thanks for saving his life so he could go home. Tears would run down my face and I would get a lump in my throat, knowing I was where I needed to be with my skills, helping those in need.

In the operating room we wore army issued combat jungle boots with breathing holes just above the sole and a steel plate in the sole (a guard against Punji sticks). Blood was everywhere, in the suctions, on the drapes, under the soldier, sometimes splattered on the surgeons and operating nurses, over the screen onto the anesthesia cart and anesthesia provider, and, of course, on the floor. HIV was not known in 1969 and "Universal Precautions" had a totally different meaning. After a case of massive blood loss, it was not uncommon to hose down the cement floor and our boots.

Blood seems to be better tolerated by a patient when warmed prior to transfusion. For blood warming in Vietnam we used coils running through an electric warming apparatus for small transfusions. For massive transfusions, units of blood were placed in a pan of tepid water. The American Blood Bank Association will not allow such a procedure for warming blood to be used in the United States because if the water is too hot the red blood cells can lyse (break into tiny pieces), thus becoming useless for the transfer of oxygen and the tiny pieces of red blood cells can plug up the kidneys and lungs. Since we had no other viable option we did what we had to do. We were very careful to test each pan of water with our elbow or hand to make sure some new corpsman did not fill the pan with hot water.

Blood pumps were used for the rapid administration of blood. Blood pumps were just big balloons fitted around the soft plastic blood container. Pumping up the balloon squeezed the blood container, forcing blood under pressure into the intravenous line. A large bore catheter (e.g. 12 gauge) allowed a unit of blood [250-500cc] to be given in about three minutes. Anesthesia providers were busy pumping up blood bags, changing empty blood bags for full blood bags, and monitoring vital signs. One trick during massive transfusions was to hook up two blood pumps to an extremity tourniquet. A tourniquet was usually placed around an extremity and inflated to a pressure adequate to stop circulation so the surgeon could work in a bloodless field. The inflating apparatus of the tourniquet was rigged to inflate blood bags rapidly, saving valuable time for the anesthesia provider, and rapidly infusing vital blood to the soldier. Today, because of the volumes of blood given in early liver transplants, a transfusion machine has been developed to give rapid infusions of large volumes of warmed blood.

In an effort to warm blood more rapidly and safely a trial was made using a microwave unit specifically designed for blood bags. The machine did a remarkable job if the blood bag contained a specified amount of blood. However, when blood is obtained, not all units are filled with the same amount of blood. Some contain up to 600 cc and others only 250 cc. The microwave blood warmer could not compensate for the wide range; large units were not warmed, small units got too hot and lysed the red blood cells. Microwave blood warming was a great idea but failed "field testing". I have not seen the technique re-introduced.

The majority of the anesthesia provider's time during surgery was concentrated in giving blood and fluids. Blood was given in large quantities. It was commonplace to give anywhere from five to fifteen units of blood to a wounded soldier. A massive transfusion in the United States is considered to be greater than10 units, in Vietnam it was greater than 30 units. We were the busiest hospital in the southern half of South Vietnam because our staff had a wide depth of surgical specialties. Wounded soldiers with the most severe injuries were routed to our hospital. Soldiers injured by a land mine might have both legs blown off, one arm blown off, the spleen ruptured, the pelvis shattered on one side or the other, possibly a liver tear, both eyes damaged, internal chest injuries, and severe damage to the face, e.g. lower jaw blown off. Multiple injuries like this in the same soldier is best approached by using teams of surgeons operating at the same time and an anesthesia provider who knows how to give thirty units of blood in one hour. Sometimes a soldier required over 100 units of blood during a case; my personal record was 108 units to one soldier. Most soldiers with such severe injuries did not make it off the operating room table alive.

Humans have four blood types: O, A, B, and AB. The vast majority of American soldiers were O Rh⁺ blood type. When a soldier required A, B, or AB blood type and only O Rh⁺ blood (called the universal blood donor blood type) was available, the practice would be to administer the O Rh⁺ blood. If the soldier received more than six units of O Rh⁺ blood, he did not receive his type specific blood for the next six months. This technique allowed us to proceed in a crisis and not worry about the consequences of blood reactions. "Dog tags" are stamped with the blood type of the soldier, enabling quick identification of blood type in a crisis and allowing bypassing the time required to type the blood. Whenever possible the soldier's blood was typed in the laboratory and crossed to the units of whole blood to be given the soldier. Only whole blood was used during my tour of duty. When fresh frozen plasma or platelets were required the request was sent to the in-country blood bank on Long Binh post.

After receiving approximately ten units of whole bank blood the soldier might develop the "red ink" syndrome. Stored bank blood loses the ability to clot, causing the soldier to bleed from every wound and orifice, despite the surgeon's attempt to tie off blood vessels. The term "red ink" is befitting because unclotted, oozing, blood looks like fountain pen red ink. Two means were available to reverse a severe case of "red ink" syndrome: 1] fresh frozen plasma and platelets [when available], and 2] fresh warm whole blood. The 24th Evacuation Hospital was located within a reasonable distance of the hematology laboratory of the U.S. Army Vietnam. A telephone call generated a runner with fresh frozen plasma and platelets. Despite the magical clotting abilities of fresh frozen plasma and platelets, the very best therapy for the red ink syndrome was, and still is, warm whole blood. A walking blood bank existed within the hospital and support staffs. Most of the time the request for warm fresh blood was filled by a call to the incoming flight officer at Tan Son Nhut Air Force Base requesting a bus load of in-processing soldiers. Out processing soldiers were not asked to be donors because their blood could be tainted with malaria, hepatitis, dengue fever, and other diseases from exposure in the jungle. The in-processing soldiers readily gave blood because they knew intuitively they might be next on the operating table and some one would give blood for them. After taking the blood, it was typed, and immediately given to the bleeding soldier in the operating room.

A moment of reflection. Some hematologists persist in telling anesthesiologists that all the elements required for clotting can be obtained from the separated components of heparinized whole blood. Today it is almost impossible to give warm whole blood to a dying soldier or civilian who has developed the "red ink" syndrome. I differ with the opinion of the "experts." My experience and the experience of others in Vietnam, is that there is something in warm whole blood that is missing from all the processed cold blood products administered separately to the soldier. We saw time and time again the efficacious effects of warm whole blood stopping the "red ink" syndrome and saving the soldier's life.

Blood meant life to many wounded soldiers in Vietnam. The equipment of the USARV Blood Bank on Long Binh post included a 1,800 cubic-foot refrigerator for storage of blood, six ice making machines and two freezers for fresh frozen plasma. In Vietnam, 13,500 to 18,500 units of blood a month were transfused to 2,500 to 4,500 soldiers. Soldiers that were transfused received on the average of four to five units of blood, and some soldiers received as many as 100 units. No one failed to receive blood because there was not enough. Blood was always available in good quantities. How much the survivors of combat wounds owe to those who unselfishly donated their blood will never be known. I thank all who sacrificed blood and I can testify many loved ones have families intact because of your donation.

During the ten-month period of my tour of duty at the 24th Evacuation Hospital 12,474 units of blood were given to 2,786 soldiers along with 147 units of fresh frozen plasma and 637 fresh blood transfusions. Only 2,800 of the 12,747 blood units transfused were low titer, O, Rh+, uncrossed units. Some soldiers did not require any blood transfusion. Our usual daily routine would be considered "heroic" in the United States today; it might even make the nightly news and, for certain, would show up as an episode on some television program.

After surgery was completed, the soldier was transferred to a hospital bed and taken to the recovery room. Oxygen was available, blood pressure cuffs and stethoscopes were used, but no electrical monitors were available to the skilled nursing personnel. Occasionally in the recovery room a blood vessel would break loose, fill the chest, abdomen or wound with blood, cause a drop in blood pressure, and necessitate taking the soldier back to the operating room to control the bleeding.

Once released from the recovery room, the soldier was assigned to the general intensive care unit, the neurosurgical intensive care unit, or a surgical ward. The team of surgeons who worked on the case determined the assignment. Because the 24th Evacuation Hospital was the neurosurgical hospital for the southern half of South Vietnam, every bed in the neurosurgery intensive care unit was filled when we were taking casualties.

Evacuation of patients from the 24th Evacuation Hospital was usually by helicopter to the Military Airlift Command wing at Tan Son Nhut

Air Force Base near Saigon. Soldiers were flown from there to either U. S. military hospitals in Japan or Clark Air Force Base in the Philippines for observation, sometimes for more surgery, and then flown to a stateside military hospital. Those requiring long term care, i.e. burns, plastic surgery, paraplegics, amputees, were eventually transferred to the Veterans Hospital nearest their home offering the care they required. Soldiers with minor injuries, e.g. broken toe, gunshot wounds requiring skin sutures, were treated at the 24th Evacuation hospital and eventually sent back to their units in Vietnam.

Soldiers wounded in combat who were evacuated to the 24th Evacuation Hospital had a 98% chance of survival. My skill in anesthesia was combined with the skills of hundreds of others to accomplish the pathway of healing. The 24th Evacuation Hospital's record of medical care in the Vietnam War was one of honor, efficiency, excellence, and caring. Anesthesia was one of the specialties that made a major impact on the excellent medicine provided our soldiers. I was and am proud to have been a small cog in a big wheel.

CHAPTER 4

SAVING LIVES

MASS CASUALTY!!, A SHOUT THAT continues to strike terror in my heart. Mass casualty had a practical definition at the 24th Evacuation Hospital: The hospital holding area was full, casualties were coming out of helicopters faster than we could find places to put them, and the triage team had to start making life and death decisions, i.e. which soldiers to try and save and which soldiers were most likely to die with or without surgery. Many times the operating rooms remained open for five or six days. My longest stretch of continuous work without sleep was approximately 48-hours. I was eventually so exhausted, I went to my room and slept fourteen hours and then got up and went back to work. Mass casualties were so frequent they coalesced into a blur.

One young soldier brought to the operating room during a mass casualty has left a vivid impression on my mind. I occasionally have a nightmare in which he is the star subject. The wounded soldier arrived in the triage area with wounds that obviously had to be treated immediately in the operating room. He was bleeding profusely all over his dirt stained jungle boots and shredded fatigues. He was quickly transported to the operating room, given a muscle relaxant for paralysis, and then an endotracheal tube was passed into his trachea to provide artificial respiration and 100% oxygen. Due to his extremely critical condition, no anesthetic drugs could be given. Two teams of surgeons vigorously started to repair his multiple wounds. The soldier had experienced some kind of mine explosion at close range and survived. The explosion blew out both eyes and ruptured both tympanic membranes. A portion of his lower jaw was missing. The soldier had both upper extremities blown to pieces, requiring the removal of both arms at the shoulder. One leg was in shreds, and the other leg had no blood supply so both legs were amputated at the hip. In addition, an exploratory abdominal surgery was required to ensure the liver and spleen had not been ruptured in the blast. He also had extensive perineal wounds, requiring a supra-pubic urinary catheter to collect urine. I do not recall how long the soldier was in the operating room or how many units of blood he received. I do remember I was surprised he made it to the intensive care unit alive. He was one of many cases taken to the operating room with high hopes of saving extremities and then finding out hidden injuries were much worse than anticipated. Had we determined before surgery that both arms and legs had to be removed, he may not had been operated on. Decisions of life and death like this were a daily occurrence and were never taken lightly by anyone on the surgical team.

In the intensive care unit, the soldier had to be on a ventilator because of failing lung function secondary to the blast effect of the explosion. It was impossible to communicate with the young man. His vocal cords were blocked by the endotracheal tube, he had no hands to hold, his ear drums were gone so he could not hear, he could not see without his eyes, and we had no way to detect if he was experiencing pain, sorrow, or love. The nurses talked to him as though he had could hear, touched him to let him know someone was there, and did their best to communicate to him that he was still alive and being cared for. After a few days in the ICU, he was moved to a ward area but remained on the ventilator. Lung injuries caused by the blast continued to worsen and soon it was apparent he would not leave Vietnam alive. A difficult decision had to be made. He could be kept alive for an undetermined amount of time if we continued his ventilation and vital function support. However, such support would deprive other wounded soldiers of the ventilator he was using. The soldier's surgeon refused to turn off the ventilator because of religious reasons and he asked me for an opinion since I was managing the ventilator care. I seriously thought and pondered about what was best for the soldier under the circumstances. There is simply no yes or no answer, ethical or religious, to situations like this. Each dilemma must be faced on a one-on-one basis.

Complex events make it impossible for anyone to look back and analyze the final decision from the classroom, the pages of a book, or the niceties of a structured ethical debate. The soldier's vital functions were deteriorating, his connections with the outside world were severed, and his wounds were totally incapacitating. I made the decision to disconnect him from the ventilator. As the plug was pulled out of the socket, the spirit of the soldier ascended to God. For me a moment of duality, sad to see him die but happy to relieve his burdens; a soul-searching decision I have never regretted or had second thoughts about. In fact, the same decision had to be made for other severely wounded soldiers with no hope for recovery in Vietnam and who would never have survived an attempt to transport them from Vietnam to the United States.

Healthcare workers, i.e. medics, doctors and especially anesthesia providers, have the privileged opportunity to share what could be the last waking moments with a wounded soldier before they go under the knife. A repeated heart-breaking moment that never got easier and still brings tears as I write these words was to answer the question "Doc, am I going to make it? Sometimes these were the last words of a mortally wounded soldier; words you heard, not his sweetheart, his wife, nor his Mom and Dad, but **you**. What would you say to the soldier if one leg was blown off at the knee, the other leg in shreds hanging from mid-thigh, and the plastic bag, neatly taped to the abdomen by the medic, was full of intestines? The only words of comfort and love that left my lips were "Yes, you will make it and go home."

Nurses, mostly female, with their special tender loving care were a Godsend to wounded soldiers. When wounded soldiers woke up with a leg gone or a penis mutilated, many did not want to go home and face a wife or sweetheart. Wounds were sometimes disfiguring, i.e. parts of jaws gone, eyes missing; wounds seen daily by us, but what about the folks at home? Our nurses were compassionate, caring, and genuinely concerned with the welfare of the soldiers. I marveled at how they could work day in and day out in such a quagmire of blood and tears and still maintain a posture of happiness and cheerfulness around the wounded soldiers. I know some who cried, just like me, in the quiet of their hooch.

The resiliency of the human spirit is marvelous. It cannot be approximated nor eradicated, and expresses itself with such a positive force to overwhelm even the skeptic. United States soldiers in Vietnam came from every walk of life. Every state, every ethnic background, every level of education, every hometown, every opinion, every hope and aspiration, were represented. As a whole, soldiers faced death with courage and hope. Remember, by the time a soldier arrived at the 24th Evacuation Hospital the war as a fantasy had ended: they were now wounded; pain and blood had replaced fantasy with reality. Each wounded soldier had to struggle with the big question: Will I survive and make it home? Waiting in the holding area prior to surgery revealed the true nature of the American soldier. Many cried, others were silent, some wanted a smoke, a few asked for a priest or rabbi, but it seemed all knew the doctors and nurses taking care of them were going to do their very best to keep them alive. Sometimes actual words of thanks were spoken but most of the time the feeling of trust was conveyed by a facial expression, an exchange of glances, the touch of the hand, or the expressed relief of being out of the jungle for a few hours.

Arriving casualties were quickly evaluated by a triage officer. The triage officer was always a surgeon who had acquired a certain expertise in trauma at the 24th Evacuation Hospital. Bandages applied in the field by the medics were removed, a quick physical examination was done to estimate the extent of injuries, and a judgment was made as to what needed to be done and how soon. Sometimes it was very obvious the soldier had to go directly to the operating room. Other times it was prudent to get an x-ray, or a consult, before a surgical plan could be determined. Previously triaged wounded were re-evaluated every time new casualities arrived to make sure those who needed immediate surgery would be taken care of first. Admission to the operating room was very important to life and certain priorities had to be set down when things got really tight. The following was a rule of thumb: American soldiers first, United Nations soldiers and Vietnamese soldiers next, then Vietnamese civilians, Viet Cong, and last, Viet Cong sympathizers. Extent of injury took precedent over the soldiers' origin, for instance, if a Viet Cong soldier came in with an injury requiring immediate attention and there was a room opening in a few minutes, then the Viet Cong soldier would be taken in ahead of an American soldier with a broken ankle who could wait without compromise.

The neurosurgeons had the most difficult decisions to make in regards to order of care. The 24th Evacuation Hospital was the neurosurgical referral hospital for the entire southern half of South Vietnam. Some wounded soldiers were referred for neurosurgical care with only superficial scrapes to the scalp while others had little brain function left. Only two neurosurgeons at a time were assigned to the hospital during most of my tour of duty. Neurosurgeons worked call shifts of 24 hours on and 24 hours off. When casualties were heavy the neurosurgeon on call worked the entire 24 hours and did anywhere from 6 to 11 craniotomies. As a comparison, civilian neurosurgeons in the United States would be considered overworked if they did two or three craniotomies in 24 hours. The wounded soldier for neurosurgery was put to sleep, then a rapid but adequate prep was done, the skull was opened, and the injured brain was literally sucked out. Once the injured tissue was removed, the bleeding stopped, a quick inspection was made to make sure no hidden injuries were present, and the skull was closed. Next patient.

Since the level of injury was so variable the neurosurgeons had worked out a system of trauma injury classification. If the brain injury was extremely critical and the soldier was neurologically intact, that is they responded appropriately to the pins and needles the neurosurgeon probed them with, then they were put in the surgery line-up. However, if the brain injury was extensive and they failed the "pins and needle" test, then they were put in the expectant category. Expectant meant they would most likely die within 24 hours with or without surgery. Expectant soldiers were given intravenous fluids, placed behind a screen, and re-evaluated by the neurosurgeon every 6 to 8 hours. Most expectant soldiers died within a few hours, occasionally we took one to surgery, but the outcome was dismal.

Gunshot wounds to the head were some of the most heartbreaking cases done at the 24th Evacuation Hospital. Many soldiers arrived conscious with good vital signs. Surgery seemed to be successful, yet some did not wake up or woke up and went into coma due to increased intracranial pressure. The intracranial pressure increased because the brain injury triggered the swelling of tissues. Sometimes the injury responded to therapy but in an unpredictable fashion. One technique used to decrease the swelling of the brain was to hyperventilate the soldier to a low carbon dioxide level, a level associated with lesser blood volume in the brain and perhaps enough to lower intracranial pressure below a critical level.

Due to the high volume of neurosurgical cases a neurosurgical intensive care unit was required. Nurses in the neurosurgical ICU were given on-the-job training to better care for these very complex cases. My job was to make rounds twice a day on soldiers requiring ventilator support. Frequently the neurosurgeons and I had to decide who was a good survival risk and, therefore, maintain ventilator support, and who had a very low chance of surviving and, therefore, stop ventilator support. Brain injuries are unpredictable in outcome on the short-term basis and many soldiers were sent to Japan and eventually the United States without us ever knowing their final outcome.

On two occasions that I recall, the United States Government allowed family members of two critically injured soldiers to come to the 24th Evacuation Hospital in Vietnam to see their son. In both cases their son was comatose, on a ventilator in the neurosurgical intensive care, with tubes coming out of every orifice, bandages on more places than just the head, and in a room with six to eight other seriously injured soldiers. I do not know what strings the parents pulled to get to Vietnam, nor do I know why they had to come. I do know I thought it was irresponsible for the Army to allow such a visit. My morale plummeted when I saw the mother of one of the soldiers holding her dying son in the middle of a war. It is no wonder military commanders since time began have not allowed mothers to be present on the battlefield during the dying moments of their son's life.

Why did the 24th Evacuation Hospital have such a sterling record of care? A number of factors came together at the same time to allow such a phenomenon. Some of the things I allude to will be challenged by others but my impressions were, and still are, founded on my own day-to-day experience. So here goes, from the eyes, ears, and brain of a 24th Evacuation Hospital anesthesiologist. Doctors and nurses were dedicated to the care of wounded soldiers and not to their individual wants. Yes, they did play when there was time, but no one I worked with ever complained of the long hours and constant exposure to pain, suffering, and death. A bond of trust and common expectations existed. You knew you were doing what you had trained to do. Everyone sensed the members of the team were working, not for any financial gain, but to save lives. Any doctor or nurse could have easily tripled or quadrupled their military salary, just from the hours worked alone. The United States government paid the soldier, the nurse, the doctor for a 24-hour day, 7 days a week, 365 days a year salary and expected each to work 24 hours a day when it was necessary. Doctors and nurses worked as a team, did the same kind of surgery repeatedly, and knew each other's techniques. Most of the wounds were described on the TV program *Mash*, as "bread and butter surgery." No fancy stuff, get in and get out with the least amount of damage to the soldier. This in no way implies delicate surgery was not preformed when it was required; our surgeons had a very high level of skill and could do anything necessary under given conditions. Practice of the same thing day and night fine-tuned the team to give the best performance of their life. No one returned to the United States to ever achieve such a record again. Even the very best trauma hospitals in the world today, with all the diagnostic tools, whistles and bells, have not achieved the same level of care. The soldiers were young, in good health prior to injury, the surgical team was fine-tuned, and appropriate resources were in place at the right time for maximal effectiveness.

Heroic efforts were the expected, not the rarity. A good example: on one occasion three extreme critical soldiers were being followed closely in the holding area waiting for an operating room to open. One had a gunshot wound to the chest but appeared stable. He suddenly collapsed and vital signs indicated a condition called pericardial tamponade. Blood had entered the envelope that surrounds the heart and was restricting the filling and emptying of the heart. This condition would have caused his death within minutes but a young surgeon in the holding area took a knife, slit a six inch opening between two ribs on the left side of his chest [no anesthesia], put his hand inside the chest, cut the pericardium envelope, and let the blood gush out from around the soldier's heart. The soldier immediately perked up, vital signs returned to normal, and he was the next candidate for the operating room.

One day I was walking through the holding area between cases and noted one soldier with a gunshot wound of the face was having obvious breathing difficulty. His lower jaw had been completely blown off, over 95% of his tongue was gone, and you could see the movement of his epiglottis. As I passed his bed he began choking on the blood oozing from the horrible wound. I could see he would soon be overwhelmed with blood in his trachea and would die before we could get him to the operating room.

I grabbed the nearest endotracheal tube, put my fingers on his epiglottis, and inserted the endotracheal tube directly into his trachea. The epiglottis protects the trachea from foreign objects under normal conditions but in this case it acted as a landmark for me to know where to put the tube to save his life. Once the tube was in place, he relaxed and breathed without difficulty. We took him to the operating room, repaired his gunshot wound, and made a hole (tracheostomy) in the trachea for breathing. He was later flown to the United States and most likely underwent extensive plastic surgery to have a new lower jaw made out of the bones of his ribs.

When a soldier arrived in the triage area without a palpable blood pressure, a very rapid heart rate, and evidence of profuse blood loss, it was imperative to start an intravenous line for immediate and rapid transfusion. Massive loss of blood causes the peripheral veins to collapse and sometimes access to peripheral veins via a needle is almost impossible. At the 24th Evacuation Hospital the large vein just under the clavicle called the subclavian vein became our primary target for massive transfusion cases. The large subclavian vein carries blood from the head back to the heart and is surrounded by tissue that keeps it from collapsing, even during massive blood loss. A technical problem can be encountered in getting the needle and catheter inside the vein. Everyone in the receiving area was taught to place lines in the subclavian veins because of the many lives it saved. Many important anatomical neighbors are found in and around the subclavian vein, i.e. subclavian artery, thoracic duct [left side only], and cupula of the lung. Getting the needle in the wrong place can trigger a chain of events just as deadly as the initial wound. It was not unusual to place a subclavian line, take the patient directly to the operating room, and then be faced with air in the chest compressing the lungs and heart. The needle for the subclavian vein had punctured the lung causing a condition known as pneumoperitoneum [continuously increasing pressure around the lung]. Once the problem was diagnosed a large needle was put in the chest, hissing was noted as the air left, and then a chest tube with a one-way valve was placed for a few days until the hole in the lung healed over. The neurosurgeons eventually became disenchanted with dealing with the post operative care of the chest tube and requested soldiers with isolated gunshot wounds to the head be spared a subclavian line and, even though chest tubes were relatively rare, we obliged them. After the war, even though I successfully placed multiple subclavian lines, I quit putting in subclavian lines because it has always been my contention the procedure should not be done unless you are doing them on a regular basis. I see too many surgeons who do three or four placements and then consider themselves experts. Better to abandon the ego trip and do what is best for the patient.

During the nine-month period from 1 December 1969 to 1 September 1970, 128 soldiers required postoperative ventilator support for an average of 9.2 days. Routinely the soldiers were monitored for two days with two arterial blood gases daily and simple pulmonary mechanics. This was followed by daily blood and pulmonary measurements for the next three days, and at least every other day for the duration of respiratory support. Not a big task in a well-staffed civilian hospital with lots of support but a labor-intensive job in a war zone. Frequent monitoring paid off in good soldier care because of early detection of pulmonary problems. Therapy was started early, thus avoiding what could have been a disaster. Routine measurement of lung compliance eventually became an integral part of improved care for postoperative pulmonary insufficiency. Due to lack of sophisticated equipment for measuring lung compliance we had to do a little "inventing" of our own. We developed a simple, inexpensive device put together with a few items normally found in anesthesia departments at the time. Nothing with any research accuracy but sufficient to detect changes in the status of the lung.

Our inhalation therapy personnel played an important role in providing life saving care to seriously injured soldiers. In addition to anesthesia, I was responsible for the inhalation therapy service in the hospital. It took a great deal of arm twisting and begging to bring together a small group of inhalation therapists. We trained medical corpsmen on-the-job to be respiratory therapists. This required me to give didactic lectures covering basic cardiopulmonary anatomy and physiology, blood gas interpretations, nebulization concepts, volume and pressure-limited respirators, and other related subjects. The few trained respiratory therapists taught the on-the-job corpsmen to use IPPB equipment, clean and maintain equipment, how to re-supply, and techniques of inhalation therapy. Respiratory therapists were always a critical need and to enhance respiratory therapy for wounded soldiers it was necessary to train the nurses on the ward to give treatments and "pinch-hit." I held in-service discussions on the ward instructing personnel in: 1] the principles of pressure-limited and volume-limited ventilators, 2] how to suction the endotracheal tube or tracheostomy without causing hypoxia, 3] why a certain respirator is chosen for a specific disease process, 4] doses and techniques for controlling the patient on the respirator with morphine sulfate, d-tubocurarine, and tranquilizers, and 5] an appreciation and respect for respirators and the dangers involved in their use. For the two-month period of November 1969 to December 1969, an average of 321 treatments per month were given by each therapist, a tremendous work-load considering the circumstances. When 24-hour coverage was started in the Intensive Care Units, respiratory therapists worked an average of 72-84 hours per week in addition to standing guard duty, being duty driver, etc. During the six-month period, January 1970 to June 1970, the average number of treatments per month per therapist rose to 651 and during May and June of 1970, when the hospital was running at capacity, each therapist averaged over 1000 treatments per month!! The members of the inhalation therapy service and nurses rendering respiratory care on the ward were proud to know their work paid off: there was an overall decrease in IPPB equipment damage, treatments were given as prescribed by the physicians, cleaner and better maintenance was done on the equipment, and there was a significant decrease in the number of patients dying respiratory deaths.

Postoperative pulmonary insufficiency was responsible for over 22 % of postoperative deaths, exceeded only by the 42% related to head injuries. It was apparent to our two thoracic surgeons and myself that the 24th Evacuation Hospital needed an intensive care unit to improve respiratory care and save lives. During the period from November 1969 to September 1970 the 24th Evacuation Hospital averaged 953 admissions per month with 385 major operations per month. At any given time 16 to 25 per cent of the patients were listed as seriously ill or very seriously ill, and an average of nine were being provided ventilator support. Wounded soldiers stayed with us an average of six to eight days before evacuation to Japan with an individual range of 1 to 62 days.

Trying to set up distinct intensive care units was met with some resistance at first. The military medical care system is a unique mixture of rigidity and flexibility. On the one hand military jargon and regulations said *An evacuation hospital is not authorized (to have) an intensive care unit* but on the other hand the chief nurse, with a twinkle in her eye, pointed out we were not breaking any regulations if we set up a system of *graduated nursing care.* Graduated nursing care allowed us to put all surgical patients on ventilators on one ward and, in effect, establish an intensive care unit without the title. Making the switch was not easy. Nurses had to be trained, additional wiring was installed to power the ventilators, and oxygen cylinders were a major problem. The nicety of piped oxygen was non-existent in Vietnam except in the "model" Army hospital in Saigon. One corpsman was kept busy moving up to fifty heavy oxygen cylinders per day.

Six months after "opening" the ICU it became obvious intensive care had enormously improved patient outcome. The Chief Army surgeon for Vietnam, a one-star general, noted the improvement in care during his weekly inspection visits. His rank and support protected us from challenge by other visiting inspectors. The ICU emphasis cut the death rate from postoperative pulmonary insufficiency by 54% in six months. Such an improvement was the result of the combined efforts of many professionals united in a desire to provide optimal patient care.

Some Interesting Cases and Innovations

On routine morning rounds in the intensive care unit an awake soldier on the ventilator burst his right carotid artery as we were talking to him! The surgeon standing next to me, immediately put pressure on the artery and we took the soldier directly to the operating room where a successful repair of the right carotid artery was accomplished. As to the cause of the rupture, no mechanism was ever found.

One particular brain injury, a penetrating wound of the dural sinus, seen perhaps once in the career of a civilian neurosurgeon, was encountered on a more frequent basis in Vietnam. The dural sinuses drain the venous blood from the brain and torn rents in the leaves of the sinus are very difficult to repair with a resultant high mortality. A penetrating wound of the dural venous sinus is difficult to repair because of extremely high blood loss, poor visualization of the tear, and massive swelling of the brain resulting from secondary venous obstruction. A neurosurgeon, John Kapp, M.D., devised an internal shunt to improve the technique of repairing a penetrating wound of the dural sinus. A mechanical internal shunt was constructed from a special child anode endotracheal tube. An anode tube is made of latex molded around a wire coil. On each end of the short tube was placed a small inflatable cuff. The inside of the tube was siliconized to prevent blood coagulation and then the tube was washed and gas sterilized. This "shunt tube" was placed in both functioning ends of the dural sinus wound by the neurosurgeon, then both cuffs inflated. The shunt tube, thus inflated, effectively moved blood away from the dural sinus tear and maintained near normal venous drainage of the brain. Now the neurosurgeon could see the tear and make a repair under direct visualization. In one of our cases the tear was not repairable but because of the shunt the neurosurgeon was able to safely take enough time to reconstruct the venous sinus with an autogenous vein graft.

The anode endotracheal tube cut blood loss in penetrating wounds of the dural venous sinuses from 5,000 to 10,000 cc per case to approximately 1000 cc per case. During the case involving placement of the autogenous vein graft no visible brain swelling was noted during a shunt time of forty-five minutes. In addition, the grafted area of the sinus was pulsating [a good sign] with the respiratory cycle and distended if digital pressure was applied to the sinus distal to the graft [another good sign].

Elective surgery was allowed when casualties stopped for a few days. Surgeons have a tendency to go stir crazy if they are denied the privilege of cutting. One elective case of special interest to me was a 36-year-old Vietnamese Army physician initially evaluated in Saigon by the U.S. Army internists for intermittent hypertension. Suspicions pointed to a pheochromocytoma, an uncommon tumor usually found in the adrenal gland. On the twenty-third day of hospitalization in Saigon, he developed acute pain in the lower right side of his abdomen and was evacuated to the 24th Evacuation Hospital because of our surgeon specialists. Initially the working diagnosis was acute appendicitis but with the past history of suspected pheochromocytoma we decided to be prepared for something unusual. A femoral artery catheter (a rare event since we had to borrow the one pressure transducer owned by the Walter Reed Army Institute of

Research), a continuous electrocardiogram, a central venous catheter, and an esophageal stethoscope were used for monitoring. A large amount of blood poured out of his abdomen when the incision entered the abdominal cavity. No acute appendicitis in this case!! Blood was infused rapidly to keep his blood pressure from falling through the floor. Surgeons sucked out as much blood as possible and immediately explored the abdomen. The right adrenal gland was found to have a very rare condition called hemorrhagic necrosis, the pheochromocytoma had ruptured, was now bleeding, and was removed. The patient recovered rapidly and left the hospital 18 days after surgery. A review of the medical literature found the operative mortality for unsuspected hemorrhagic necrosis of a pheochromocytoma to be in the range of 50%. Our success in handling such a rare case in a war zone was due to our expertise in trauma management.

Another innovation introduced was the use of sterile water under pressure to debride wounds embedded with shredded pieces of uniform, grass, and other debris carried into the wound by a penetrating object, i.e. bullet, mine fragments, etc. The equipment was a modified version of the gadget used to clean teeth and proved to be quite efficient for cleansing the wound quickly. Water pressure debridement had one obvious drawback: the floor was covered with water, blood, and debris.

Somehow a very, very, obese Sergeant (In peacetime he would have been involuntary discharged) had found his way to Vietnam and was assigned to the hospital staff. The first time I saw him, I prayed he would never get sick and come to the operating room because I had no idea how we could ventilate him after an operation. Well, he developed appendicitis, had an appendectomy, and because of his morbid obesity, required ventilator care for a number of days after surgery. A couple of weeks before his appendectomy the hospital had acquired a very sophisticated ventilator from one of the old French hospitals in Saigon. Engstromâ, a European firm, made the unit and no one at the hospital knew how to run it. I had heard of the machine but had never seen one or used one. It took me about three days to figure out how the machine worked [no manual] and it turned out to be a lifesaver for the Sergeant. Two anesthesia providers wheeled the monster sized Engstromâ ventilator into the operating room, ventilated the Sergeant during the case, and then transferred the ventilator and Sergeant to the postoperative care ward. I must admit the Engstromâ ventilator was an answer to my prayer because none of our other ventilators would have been able to ventilate a man of his size.

A Vietnamese soldier, with a live grenade lodged in his liver, was evacuated from the battlefield by a Vietnamese Army helicopter and brought to the helipad of the 24th Evacuation Hospital. Not being a weapons expert, I did not understand how such a thing could happen. Someone explained the grenade had been shot from a rifle and usually the grenade blew up on contact. In this case the grenade did not explode on contact but had penetrated the skin of the abdomen, lodged in the liver, and was considered to be live ammunition. Since the helicopter was Vietnamese Army, many wanted the wounded soldier flown to the Vietnamese Army hospital in Saigon. But since he had arrived safely and it was uncertain what would happen if he were moved again, it was decided to keep him. Our solution to minimize damage in case of an explosion was to set up an operating room on the helipad. During a quick meeting of the anesthesia and surgical staff, one unmarried CRNA and one unmarried surgeon volunteered. A three to four foot wall of sandbags was built around an operating table at the far end of the helipad, away from the hospital. A small window was left in the wall for the anesthesia provider to have access to the soldier's head. The operating staff wore flack jackets, steel pots, and any other protective device that did not interfere with their work. Once the wounded soldier was asleep the surgeon removed the grenade *very carefully* from the liver, handed it off to the bomb squad, and proceeded to stop the bleeding. The live grenade was taken to a distant safe spot and detonated. The Vietnamese soldier survived the surgery and after a short recovery was evacuated to Saigon. About two weeks later the 24th Evacuation Hospital Commander awarded each participant a special medal for action above and beyond the call of duty. I was certainly impressed with everyone's devotion to duty and consideration for an allied soldier. Motto: Just take care of what needs to be done to save a life, let whatever follows take care of itself.

By 1968 a rare deadly syndrome, malignant hyperthermia, had been recognized by the anesthesia community. Healthy patients without any history of previous disease would very rapidly develop fevers as high as 108-110°F in one to two hours when exposed to some of the drugs used in anesthesia. High temperature was a symptom of massive disruption of cellular membranes taking place throughout the body. It seemed like the body was a gun cocked and waiting to fire, all it needed was the right anesthetic drug to pull the trigger. In 1969 therapy for malignant hyperthermia was dismal, mortality was 100%. After the Vietnam War a drug called Dantrolene was found to stop the syndrome and today if treatment is initiated rapidly, mortality is nil. Only one wounded soldier during my year at the 24th Evacuation Hospital developed malignant hyperthermia. He came in with a penetrating gunshot wound of the neck. Vital signs were stable, but the prudent thing to do was to explore the wound to rule out injury to the carotid artery. Immediately after the induction of general anesthesia, his temperature started to rise. We had used succinylcholine [a muscle relaxant], and halothane [a general anesthetic]; both drugs later determined to be capable of triggering malignant hyperthermia. The wounded soldier was packed in ice and ice water was pumped into his stomach in an effort to reduce the high fever. Eventually his temperature did come down but he had suffered an indeterminate amount of brain damage from the high body fever. Two days later he went into kidney failure and was evacuated to Saigon for treatment on the only kidney dialysis unit in Vietnam. Every day we called to see how he fared. About five days later, he died. A tragedy.

One wounded soldier warranted bypassing the usual evacuation route: 1) arrival at the hospital by helicopter, 2) triage, 3) operating room, 4) ICU or ward, 5) helicopter to Ton Son Nhut AFB, 6) Military Airlift Command to one of the army hospitals in Japan or the Philippines, and finally 7) the homing bird to the United States. This soldier was returning from a night patrol when he was caught in a "mad-minute" of gunfire from his own troops. A shell had been fired in his direction that sprayed a large area with multiple, small, rapidly traveling, steel arrows. One of the steel arrows penetrated his chest, entered one of the heart chambers, and lodged in the cordae tendinae (small fibers holding the heart valve in place). The small puncture wound in the heart had spontaneously closed preventing blood from entering the pericardial sac surrounding the heart. On arrival at the 24th Evacuation Hospital he was alert, stable, and doing very well. The entry wound was apparent. Lateral and frontal chest x-rays showed the arrow in the heart. What to do? If the arrow dislodged it might pass out of the heart valve and cause serious damage. Obviously the arrow could not be removed without a heart-lung machine; the nearest one: Tripler Army Medical Center in Hawaii. A stunned American soldier was soon loaded on a helicopter, transferred to an awaiting Military Airlift Command airplane at Ton Son Nhut AFB and flown non-stop to Tripler Army Medical Center where the heart-lung machine and surgical team awaited him. Expensive? No doubt!! Saved his life? Without question!! Spinoffs from this heroic effort were a lifting of morale in the troops in Vietnam (success stories like this traveled very fast) and a feeling amongst the medical personnel that our soldiers were getting the best care in the world.

Not all treatment was successful. Some died despite all that could be done. Occasionally human error was responsible for a death due to fatigue, inattention to detail, and/or misjudgment. Only once do I recall a patient dying because of physician's lack of knowledge. An elderly North Vietnamese woman was brought to the hospital with a large open wound of the tibia and fibula on the left leg. The wound had been treated with maggots by the Viet Cong. When the leg was unwrapped, the wound was found to be glistening, clean, and basically ready for a secondary closure. The woman did not have a fever or any other sign of infection. However, one of our surgeons felt the woman needed to be treated with an antibiotic. He ordered a very large dose of penicillin that had a potassium molecule attached to each molecule of penicillin. The ordered dose of penicillin far exceeded what was needed for the patient, a fact brought to the attention of the surgeon by the nurse. As many surgeons do, he told the nurse he was the doctor, she was only a nurse, give the dose. The penicillin was infused into the vein, resulted in an overdose of potassium, her heart stopped beating, and we could not resuscitate her. Our surgeon's arrogance and lack of knowledge about potassium being linked to the penicillin caused a needless death.

Transporting a critically ill soldier on a helicopter is no piece of cake. Rotor noise drowns out all normal conversation, as well as, blood pressure sounds, heart sounds, and any conversation with the wounded soldier. Huey evacuation helicopters were not equipped with any kind of physiological monitor so you had to resort to a finger on the pulse, skin and nail bed color, counting and watching respirations, and a general impression of how the soldier was doing. I was blessed with transporting soldiers who had been operated on and were somewhat stable. I cannot even conceive of the nightmare faced by a medic in the field who accompanied soldiers bleeding to death.

A few combat soldiers shot themselves in the foot or otherwise mutilated themselves, in order to obtain a ticket home. How many soldiers self-inflicted wounds is not known because all casualties were officially categorized as wounded in action, accident, or other legitimate casualty classification. In addition to self-inflicted wounds, we received senior sergeants and officers who had been shot by our own troops. These officers and sergeants were apparently deemed guilty of risking men's lives needlessly for their own career advancement, i.e. body counts, or had abused the privileges of higher rank. Usually the circumstances of the soldier's wound were not evident when they arrived but the events leading to the shooting sometimes filtered in later. Our job was not to judge, just fix the wounded soldier and let the military sort out the dirty details. What a senseless waste of life; some destroyed, some maimed.

Many capable internists and general medical officers were busy on the medical wards and clinics of the 24th Evacuation Hospital. Physicians found diseases they had only read about in medical school and some they had to look then up in reference books. Names like dengue and Tasakasihi fever were new. The usual tropical diseases, i.e. parasite invasions and malaria, were indigenous to Vietnam but expected.

Whenever possible the team approach was used by the surgeons on multiple injury cases. Getting the bleeding stopped and the soldier out of the operating room as soon as possible was imperative for success. Sometimes I would look over the drapes and see a team of orthopedic surgeons working on the legs, a team of general surgeons with the abdomen open, and a plastic or ENT surgeon doing something on the face. Of course, a team faced with the acute crisis of getting the bleeding stopped would begin the case. Once bleeding was controlled, the other teams would join the fracas. Teamwork was something seen in Vietnam on a regular basis but something I find to be blatantly absent in civilian practice. Time and time again the maxim has been proven: To give the soldier/patient the best chance of survival it is necessary to get them to the operating room as soon as possible to stop the bleeding and then get them out of the operating room as soon as possible. Delay in taking soldiers/patients to the operating room because of needless x-rays and laboratory studies is inexcusable. In combat, multiple surgical teams working at the same time saved lives. In stateside hospitals the common practice is to have one surgical specialty work at a time, i.e. a general surgeon controls the bleeding and closes, followed by the orthopedic surgeon who works and closes, and then the plastic surgeon putters around for three to four hours and finally closes; a practice that definitely increases morbidity and mortality.

At no time in my forty-year medical career have I experienced such a oneness in the operating team as during my tour of duty in Vietnam. No surgeons complained about "turnover time" between cases nor did they gripe about not being able to get their patient on the operating room schedule to fit their vacation or golf game. No one was incriminating someone else for the problems in the operating room. The surgeons, the anesthesia providers, and the operating room nurses and technicians were united as one to serve the wounded soldiers. I must admit this unity has been sometime I have yearned for in civilian practice. The constant bickering between the anesthesia providers, the surgeons, and the operating nurses is not pleasant and leads to a consistent dead-end. The lay public has no idea of the contention existing in most operating rooms; a contention that is not necessary but is present because the surgeons must "keep control" of everyone, the anesthesia providers are exerting their "control", and the operating nurses are trying to "control" the schedule to get out after an eight-hour shift.

CHAPTER 5

PEOPLE

MANY OF THOSE ASSIGNED TO the 24th Evacuation Hospital would have made great character sketches for the old *Readers Digest* "My Most Unforgettable Character" series. A war had once again brought together a wide range of personalities with diverse backgrounds, education, morals, patriotism, and devotion to duty.

Except for the real bullets, live grenades, and bloodied soldiers, the 24th Evacuation Hospital was a reproduction of the television series "Mash" even though high-ranking medical corps officers in the Army did not particularly want it to be. Most the nurses and physicians were civilians drafted for two years, one year being spent in Vietnam. The majority of "regular" Army officers, called "lifers", like myself, were young and inexperienced in leadership and organizational abilities. When the civilian/ military mix came together, something magical happened. Military ranks faded away and getting the job done became the order of the day. Physicians in Vietnam did not have to establish a reputation in order to attract "new business." It was a change of pace to see the surgeons, especially, act as professionals without all the posturing for position and power seen continually in civilian practice. The exceptions to those devoted to excellence could be numbered on the fingers of one hand. My memories of fellow workers are positive, comforting, and, above all, heartwarming. Men and women dedicated to taking care of wounded soldiers, sometimes at the risk to their own health. Concerns for status, physical and mental, were disregarded as everyone lowered heads and charged into the fracas of gore. War is not what most movies make it out to be. If I were to choose one movie about Vietnam depicting the real dichotomy of love and hate it would have to be *Platoon.*

Our youth, energy, devotion, and professionalism sustained the work. Initially you were frightened that it would be impossible to handle such great responsibility but after a few weeks the shock of seeing a steady diet of blood and guts subsided. In training I was exposed to minimal trauma but did not have a steady diet of trauma as experienced continually in Vietnam. Teamwork brought inner strength and gave you the confidence necessary to treat the wounded soldiers. First encounters with multiple traumatized soldiers made you feel like you were the dull edge of a knife trying to cut paper. Only after you had been honed, first by the coarse side of the sharpening stone and then by the fine side of the sharpening stone, to a razor sharp edge by working in the operating room, did you begin to feel comfortable and confident.

Never did you get used to the terrible sights of mutilated soldiers. Words cannot express the horrors of war experienced at the 24the Evacuation Hospital. Each doctor, nurse, and corpsman, dealt with the traumatic experience of a daily diet of horror. Some cried, some were depressed, some were angry, but most held the horror inside to erupt years later. Sharing our experiences in the hooch was a good outlet. Men, especially, bottled up the psychological trauma in order to maintain the "American Macho" image.

Lack of anesthesia personnel in the war zone required me to train American physicians fresh out of their internship to administer anesthesia. Usually non-specialty physicians were sent to a firebase for six months as a general physician and then given the opportunity to rotate to a larger hospital. If the physician requested anesthesia on-the-job training, we made good use of their skills. The end result was usually a sharp physician trained and ready to do one kind of anesthesia, e.g trauma. The U.S. trained physicians had an excellent background, spoke the language, i.e. medical and English, and were always willing to work. One physician was a standout: Dr. Will Wright. He came to us for on-the-job training after serving as a general practitioner for six months on a firebase in the northern half of South Vietnam. Dr. Wright was a man of high caliber, morally and intellectually. He acquired the technical and cognitive skills of an anesthesiologist rapidly and it was a pleasure to see him work. After the Vietnam War he came, by chance, to the University of Arizona to do a formal residency training program in anesthesia. I happened to be member of the faculty and it was such a pleasure to see him emerge as the shining star of the residency program. Dr. Wright recently retired from the practice of anesthesiology. He served his patients faithfully and with dignity. A real credit to the practice of medicine. It was my honor and privilege to know a man of such caliber.

Dr. Wright told many stories of the atrocities he experienced while on the firebase. The firebase was attacked by the Vietcong and North Vietnam Army [NVA] with mortars and waves of armed soldiers. He described how American soldiers fabricated "mad minutes" at varied times during the night to catch the enemy off guard. A "mad minute" was 60 seconds of concentrated weapons fire from designated points on the perimeter. Such firepower could easily cut a tree in half, you can imagine what it would do to enemy soldiers attempting to infiltrate who got caught in the crossfire.

About two weeks before Dr. Wright was to leave the firebase for transfer to the 24th Evacuation Hospital, the firebase Commander was ordered to close the firebase, move the troops, and build another firebase. Dr. Wright said that before the order to close the firebase had been given, the firebase had been on a list to have a new dental clinic built. The Commander had tried for months, without success, to get the construction team to come and build the dental clinic. Within days of the announcement of the firebase closure, the construction crew arrived and, despite pleas from the Commander, built a new dental clinic. The U.S. construction crew did not come under the jurisdiction of the Commander and the construction crew was determined to build the dental clinic so they could bill the U.S. government for the project. The dental clinic was completed just days before it was abandoned. Greed crushed commonsense and logic.

Arriving doctors and nurses were oriented very rapidly. New members of the anesthesia team were expected to get gear stowed and report to work the next day. Anesthesiologists and nurse anesthetists started taking call within 48 hours and on-the-job trained physicians were worked into the call schedule as soon as possible. One baptism of fire arranged for all new anesthesia personnel was the privilege to administer an anesthetic to a Vietnamese civilian. Many of the Vietnamese were infected with *Ascari*, a long worm that can grow as big as a night crawler. The *Ascari* worm sometimes takes up residence in the respiratory system. Administration of an anesthetic to an infected Vietnamese caused the *Ascari* worm to "abandon ship", crawl up the trachea, and out the mouth underneath the anesthetic mask, or out the nose. Everyone waited outside the operating room in anticipation of the blood curdling scream as the worm made its' debut. Not a common occurrence, mind you, but a memorable one when it happened!

Some men and women in any position of power feel superior to everyone else. We had our share of leaders who were "egomaniacs" and let us know in no uncertain terms that they were better than us in practice, in medical skills, in judgment, and were superior to us as human beings. Personalities like these surround themselves with those like themselves and those who will "lick the feet" of the dominant personality. The isolation of the 24th Evacuation Hospital allowed this phenomenon to fester and florish.

The Hospital Commander had chosen an older civilian surgeon drafted into the Vietnam War as Chief of Surgery. An egomaniac that felt he was superior to everyone in the hospital in training, practice, surgical skills, judgment, breeding, and basic worth as a human being. His surgical skills were reasonable but many of our surgeons had superior technical and cognitive skills. The Commander had chosen this particular surgeon as Chief of Surgery with purpose in mind; through him the Commander could control the medical staff by virtue of allowing the Chief of Surgery to suppress the physicians through direct command and intimidation. The Commander used threats of Article 15 to try and keep his medical and nursing staff in line. He was continually trying to avoid a "Mash Unit" atmosphere on his watch. The attempt did not work well. Physicians and nurses working extremely long hours every week needed and sought a release from stress.

The Hospital Commander did little to endear himself to his staff. Despite multiple roadblocks and lack of support by the Chief of Surgery, the 24th Evacuation Hospital had an excellent record; solid evidence of the devotion of the medical and nursing staff to the wounded soldiers. A couple of incidents showed the Hospital Commander's lack of leadership. One was an attempt to court martial those responsible for bringing a band to the hospital in the back of an ambulance for a party. The transportation had been arranged from the nearby motor pool and really did not come under his jurisdiction in the first place. Even if it had, he should have realized what was happening and just closed his eyes to the event. Another event was the search for the "villain" who threw rocks on his hooch in the middle of the night. Yes, it was a crude stunt by one of the physicians who was drunk and stupid, but did it merit an Article 15? Just a good dressing down, some limitations of privileges, e.g. taken off the rotation list for one rotation to accompany a patient to Japan, or perhaps a delay, not cancellation of his R & R. Sometimes you wonder how men are chosen by the military for responsible positions. Thank goodness the Peter Principle does not apply to all leadership positions in the military.

The Chief of Surgery was a character beyond belief. In my forty-five years in medicine I have never worked with a surgeon with such an ego. My experience has exposed me to some real dowsers who felt they were God's most precious gift to mankind and medicine. This surgeon was one step above the gift stage; he really believed he had the attributes of God! i.e. infallible, omnipotent, and without guile. His main purpose in life was to allow the professional staff to work with him, praise him, and recognize him as the best surgeon they would ever see in their lifetime. He had been drafted out of a very lucrative surgical practice where he had bullied everyone on the staff. From his own admission, he was "… the surgeon for the rich.", therefore, a notch above the rest of the surgeons in town. With his pull and political contacts, I never understood how he ended up in Vietnam. The military sometimes rewards soldiers who characterize themselves as great. Just before he left the Commander recommended the Chief of Surgery for the Legion of Merit, a very high honor for a non-combatant soldier. With this medal in hand he informed the Army he would give them the honor of staying on active duty if promoted to the rank of General, and he meant it. Thank goodness the rank of General has to be approved by Congress and recommendations go through certain steps before approval. Our Chief of Surgery, a Major, did not have the leadership, experience, and skills necessary to be considered a General; except in his own eyes.

I was unable to avoid an ultimate confrontation with the Chief of Surgery. During my first week I had re-organized the Respiratory

Therapy department to give 24-hour service in the hospital and to make more efficient rounds on the wards; a patient quality improvement issue. The Chief of Surgery called me to his office, sat me down and, in no uncertain terms, told me any improvements in the hospital had to be run past him and I had flagrantly bypassed his authority. He threatened to take my name off the rotation list to Japan, cancel my future R & R request, and even send me to a firebase if I did not adhere to his position of power. A moment of truth for me, should I let the man have his glory or by defying him, deprive the wounded soldiers of the only anesthesiologist at the time at the 24th Evacuation Hospital. My thoughts are still clear to me to this day: The soldiers came first, I yielded to his control in this situation, did my best to avoid him in the future, and devoted myself to the care of the wounded. When he left, we had a "departure celebration" party. The replacement Chief of Surgery did more in his first two weeks than the previous Chief had done in his entire year as "King".

"Love affairs" of convenience, lust, or just loneliness were rampant. Many of the nurses were living with surgeons. In my follow up after the war, I do not know of one love affair started at the 24th Evacuation Hospital in Vietnam that continued more than one year, despite the couple getting married after service in Vietnam. Events of the moment, loneliness, threat of death, stress, chronic fatigue, were just a few of the factors responsible for pulling a man and woman together. One surgeon was happily married with children, so he said, and was living with a lovely single nurse whom he "promised" he would divorce his wife after the war and marry her. She had filled a hope chest in his hooch with items for their wedding. I vividly recall the day he was leaving to meet his wife for R & R, tears were streaming down her cheeks as her lover boarded the helicopter. It was like the separation of man and wife when you left for Vietnam. After returning home she found out the hard way that he had no intention of making any changes in his marital status. She was heart broken.

One couple used to make love in the evenings, during lulls in casualties, in the respiratory therapy office adjacent to the Recovery Room. Things went very well with the passionate love affair during the time in Vietnam; they even went on R & R together. Follow up: Marriage and divorce within a year after they left Vietnam. Most likely reasons: Interests not the same in peacetime, disillusioned with each other, passion triggered by loneliness diminished and died, and/or denial of Vietnam and not able to switch the basis of their love to another foundation.

Arrangements for sleeping with one another were made very quickly. Two new surgeons arrived very shortly after my tour began. Both were married, both had a regular sleep-in nurse within 14 working days. Upon arrival they told us their goal was to get someone as soon as possible because they did not want to miss out on their love-making just because they were in Vietnam. To my knowledge both returned home to the wife and family left behind.

Tragic cases happened all the time. One very religious male nurse became involved with a female nurse. He was married, she was single. Frequent love making occurred with exchanges of love and admiration between them. The affair was described by the male nurse as the "real thing" but he eventually began to have very strong questions of moral transgression. His religious convictions stirred his soul with guilt as he talked of adultery and breaking a commitment to his wife. Tears of guilt, tears of a sorrowful soul, exited his eyes when he discussed the dilemma. The affair did not stop, despite religious convictions, until the single nurse rotated back to the U.S. He told his wife when he returned home. Eventually his marriage fell apart and his wife was awarded custody of the children. Years later he remarried a nurse but not to the one he had an affair with in Vietnam.

The nurses' quarters were adjacent to the hospital and surrounded by a wall with barbed wire on top; some said to keep out American men, not the enemy. One-night love affairs in the nurses quarters were not uncommon, many times the surgeons would give us the telephone number in the hall nearest the room of the affair. Helicopter pilots were constantly visiting the 24th Evacuation Hospital. Our nurses were like a magnet, drawing in males from miles around. Just like all wars.

Some drafted surgeon's had a hard time fitting into the routine of a wartime trauma hospital. The could not change their techniques to meet the needs of patients and the rapid turnover rate required to process casualties. For instance, one surgeon insisted in draping procedures intended for elective surgery in civilian hospital and could not adjust to the rapid turnover in our environment. After repeated log jams of wounded soldiers he left for the on-coming surgeons, it was decided by the medical staff and the hospital commander that he could not function in our environment. The Army eventually determined the surgeon should not practice anywhere in Vietnam and he was transferred to a Veterans Hospital stateside. His transfer and eventual replacement returned us back to our high state of efficiency and effectiveness.

One time one of our neurosurgeons was allowed to go on R & R without a temporary replacement. The remaining neurosurgeon had to take call for seven continuous days. Somehow he was able to make it but I can tell you we all did what we could to keep any cases of a frivolous nature away from him.

One of the neurosurgeons on my watch was fast and competent. All were impressed with his dedication and surgical skills. He was easy to work with and enjoyable to talk to after the work was done. No one disputed his devotion to the soldiers under his care. His downfall was a naive approach to marijuana. He told us, just before he rotated home, that on more than one occasion he had taken marijuana just before his shift of duty to see what the effects would be on his cognitive and technical skills. A stupid thing to do, but no harm apparently resulted from the experiment. We later learned he was arrested for having marijuana in his personal effects when he arrived in the U.S.

Professional anesthesia staff had personal problems. There was a chronic shortage of anesthesia personnel throughout the war. One of our anesthesia personnel had been rehabilitated from alcoholism, but the stresses of Vietnam caused him to revert back to a drink now and then. Everyone watched him very carefully to protect the soldiers and him. In my role as Chief of Anesthesia, I had to counsel him regarding his drinking. I requested he only drink in his hooch. He knew without any doubt that if he showed up in the operating for work with the smell of alcohol on his breath that he would have to submit to a blood alcohol test. If the test was positive the Army would drum him out of the service with a dishonorable discharge, causing him to lose his 19 years of dedicated service. To lose his pension was enough incentive for him to keep within the guidelines and preform his work satisfactorily.

One of the female nurse anesthetists loved to bait the surgeons and get them upset. She enjoyed swearing with and at them and her language was something else to listen to in the operating room. I came to find out very soon she was one of the most competent nurse anesthetists on the staff, was very dependable, and would work until she dropped from exhaustion when the casualties were overwhelming. She worked hard and played hard. A credit to her profession, a little too coarse to be classified as ladylike, but I grew to love her as a person who did not put on a facade. She was honest, forthright, and had character that overshadowed any bad language she might try to "stun" you with.

Medical evacuation [MedEvac] helicopter pilots and crew displayed valiant, courageous service, day and night. These men were the backbone of saving lives. Without their dedicated service it would have been impossible to get the casualties early enough to save them. The ground ambulance service of World Wars I and II and Korea had a high mortality rate. In the Korean War helicopters were used for some medical evacuations.

In Vietnam MedEvac helicopters were almost the exclusive means of patient transportation to the hospital. Helicopter pilots sometimes had to hover above the jungle canopy while a winch was lowered to lift the wounded soldier off the jungle floor 60 to 70 feet below. A hovering helicopter is a sitting target for the enemy; at night it was even more dangerous. The MedEvac helicopters were marked with a red cross designated by the Geneva Convention as non-combatant but the red cross seemed to be more of a target than a hindrance. Everyone deeply appreciated and held in awe the sacrifices made by the crews of the MedEvac helicopters. God bless the helicopter crews who died trying to save the wounded. May peace and satisfaction of a job well done find a place in the hearts of helicopter crews who returned from Vietnam safely.

Friendships in Vietnam flourished. Two nurse anesthetists I worked with in Vietnam, Ivan Dunlap, CRNA and Michael Kesler, CRNA, later joined me in anesthesia private practice. I knew without a doubt they were competent, dependable, and my friends. Both of them were closer to me than my brother. Some ask how can that be? The answer is the intense experience of war, the constant gore and horror, brought men together in a profound friendship that cannot be dissolved easily. Have I followed up on the friendships made in Vietnam? Only a few. Not because I did not want too, but because my life experiences have stood in the way.

William Clayton Petty, Major, MC, U.S. Army, reporting for duty at the 24th Evacuation Hospital, Long Binh, Vietnam, October 1969.

Long Binh post from a helicopter. You can see the temporary buildings and get an idea of just how much material and manpower was required during the war. This was a very large military post and served as headquarters for the U.S. Army in Vietnam.

The 24ᵗʰ Evacuation Hospital taken from a Huey helicopter in June 1969 by Ed Fortmiller (deceased). Photograph: Printed with permission of Mrs. Joan Formiler, 27 January 2016.

The entrance of the 24ᵗʰ Evacuation Hospital taken from a helicopter exiting the hospital. You can see the "fire extinguisher" in the foreground and the Quonset huts lined up with other building types providing the operating rooms and hospital wards.

A typical "dust-off" medical evacuation helicopter used in the Vietnam war. The dual fire extinguishers were present just in case there was a crash. Helicopter evacuation saved many lives during the Vietnam War. The helicopter pilots were brave, tenacious, and devoted to their jobs. We had great respect for the sacrifices they made to get critically wounded soldiers to us in time to save their lives. The exceptional record of the 24th Evacuation Hospital was the result of the teamwork of the helicopter pilots, the medics, and the hospital staff.

Outside the window of my "hooch." Large fifty-gallon drums were filled with sand and topped off with bags of sand to serve as deterrents to a bomb or mortar attack. The sand bags were starting to leak because of the humid weather. You can see the drapes in my window and a window air conditioner. The air conditioner serviced two rooms but I was lucky and the controls were on my side of the partition!

The Triage area. Wounded soldiers were brought in on stretchers from the helicopters. The nurses and doctors immediately evaluated the status of the wounded soldier and began the initial resuscitation. A triage surgeon determined the priority of injury and how soon the soldier would go to the operating room. Oxygen cylinders were secured to the wall and stethoscopes were hung from a pipe connected to the ceiling.

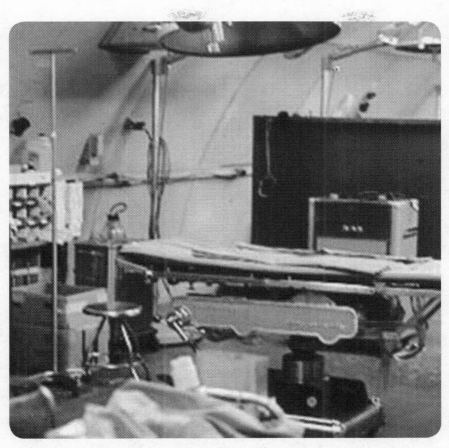

An operating room "suite." "Rooms" were merely areas partitioned off by portable panels. Each enclosure had an operating table (a real table with positioning capabilities), a Boviê (an electrical device used for hemostasis), a surgical table, poles to hold intravenous fluids and blood bags, a suction device, an anesthesia machine, and, of course, portable operating lights. We were adequately equipped for trauma surgery. The floors were concrete and were cleaned by throwing buckets of water on the floor and then mopped.

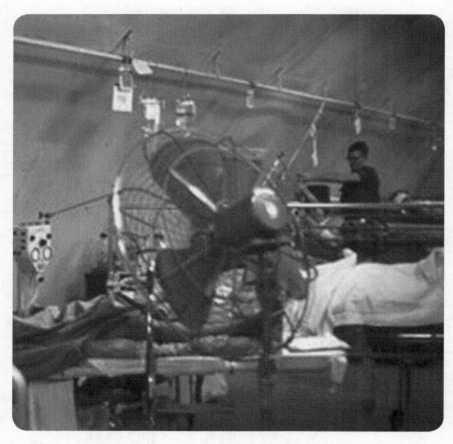

The Recovery Room. Patients were put in standard hospital beds when possible after surgery. The recovery room was a busy place and one of my jobs was to oversee the care when I was not involved in a case in the operating room. We had cylinders of oxygen secured to the walls that provided oxygen to the patients and power to drive the respirators. Sometimes it got a bit hot, despite window air conditioners so a fan was used to circulate air.

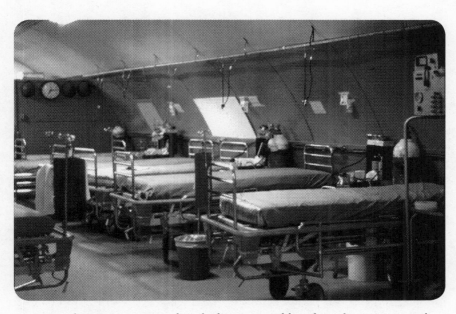

A typical post-operative ward readied to receive soldiers from the recovery ward. The stethoscopes are hung from the pipe, oxygen cylinders were secured to the wall, and the floor was clean.

My office in the surgery Quonset hut. I did not spend a great deal of time in the office but it was a nice place to go to write letters home and cool off during an exceptionally hot, humid day. We wore our combat boots, fatigue pants, and surgical tops a lot. If we were in the surgical area we usually, but not always, put on a pair of surgical scrubs.

The container designed for the Military Field Anesthesia Machine, Model 785, used during the Vietnam War by the U.S. military. The container could withstand a drop of 50 feet from a helicopter. The equipment necessary to safely administer an anesthetic to an adult was housed inside the container.

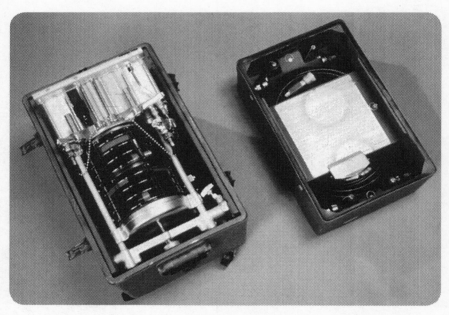

One-half of the container had the anesthesia machine (left picture) and the other half (right picture) was filled with the equipment necessary to complete a functional anesthesia machine.

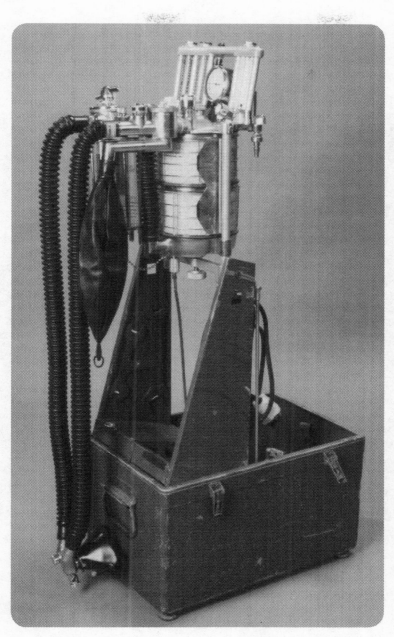

The Military Field Anesthesia Machine, Model 785, assembled and ready for use. Reusable rubber breathing tubes, masks, and rebreathing bags were used. After each case the reusables were washed thoroughly.

Control head of the Model 785 Military Field Anesthesia Machine. The flowmeter for nitrous oxide is shown on the left in blue, the flowmeter for cyclopropane is in orange next to the nitrous oxide flowmeter, and the flowmeter for oxygen is on the far right in white, the International color for oxygen.

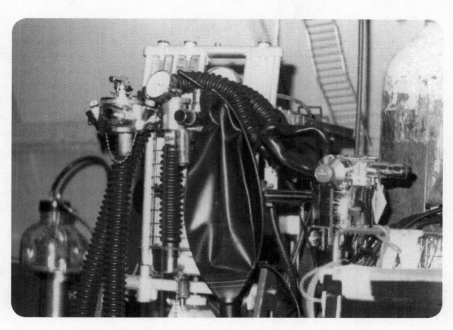

*Adaptation of a Halothane vaporizer to the control head of
the Model 785 Military Field Anesthesia Machine.*

The Birdà respirator was easy to repair and easy to learn how to use. These machines were used in the operating room to ventilate soldiers so that we could have both hands available to give the vast amounts of blood necessary for resuscitation. These machines had limitations but as long as you knew the limitations the machines were life saving.

One of the early ECG machines of modern times. These machines were basically oscilloscopes. Only one of the three major leads of the ECG could be displayed at a time and it was difficult to read the screen but once you learned how to fine-tune the signal you could make it work successfully.

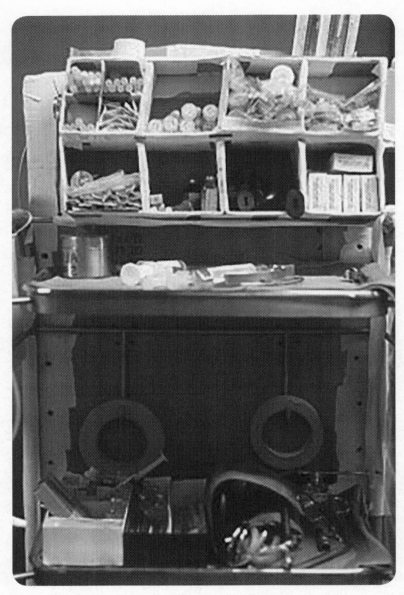

My anesthesia cart. Each anesthesia provider was given a stainless steel operating room cart to configure as an anesthesia work station. The partitions were made of cardboard covered by layers and layers of white adhesive tape. Frequently used items were stored in the compartments on the top and items like blood pressure cuffs were stored in the open areas on the bottom of the cart.

ANESTHESIA

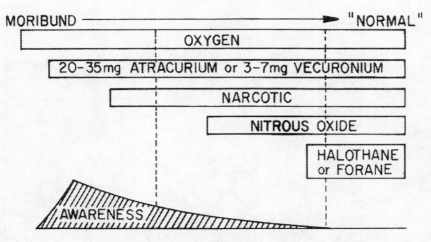

A schematic devised after I returned home to display the technique of anesthesia I used in combat casualties in Vietnam. If the patient was moribund, that is, nonresponsive to outside stimulus, had no blood pressure that could be detected by conventional means, and had a high heart rate, then the patient was given oxygen and the surgery started. If the patient moved on incision, then a muscle relaxant drug was given to keep the soldier from moving while life saving surgery proceeded. Once the bleeding was under control the blood pressure was usually detectable, the heart rate slowed, and the patient was considered to be on the way to recovery. A narcotic could then be added for pain relief. Eventually nitrous oxide, which could be reversed very easily, was added, and finally a very low amount of halothane. Each drug added during the resuscitation was given in low doses initially to make sure the soldier could withstand the changes in physiology induced by the drug. If the soldier tolerated the drug given, the dose was gradually increased, and then the next drug on the schematic was added.

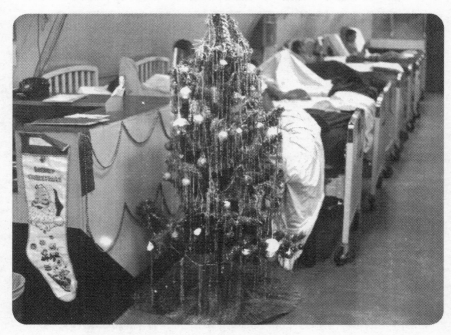

Christmas Tree and Merry Christmas stocking on a patient ward.

Santa Claus visiting an orphan in the mess hall of the 24th Evacuation Hospital. Many orphans were hosted to a great dinner, Christmas music, companionship of staff members, and a visit from Santa Claus bearing gifts.

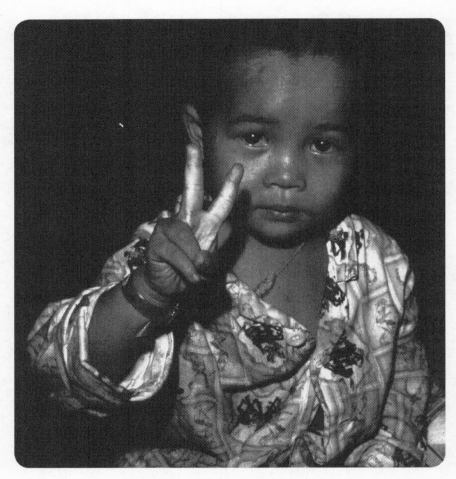

A Vietnamese child brought in for elective surgery during a lull in the war. We often did orphans who required either eye surgery or plastic surgery. You can tell the influence of the Americans on the young boy as he gives us the peace sign. Operating on these children was a pleasure and provided great satisfaction.

Zoe Leone and I on my Rest and Recreation leave in Honolulu, Hawaii.

William Clayton Petty, M.D. on a bright sunny day in front of a lovely banana tree in South Vietnam.

Dr. Buu, a South Vietnam Army Medical Officer,
and I in front of the operating room entrance.

Presentation of a token of appreciation for training Dr. Buu the basics of anesthesia. From right to left: unknown, Dr. Petty, Sargent Saun, Dr. Buu.

The University of Saigon Medical Education Center
(Medical School) in Saigon, Vietnam in 1970.

William Clayton Petty, MD

CHAPTER 6

REST AND RECREATION

In-Country

THE 24ᵀᴴ EVACUATION HOSPITAL WAS located within the confines of a large military base called Long Binh. During quiet periods we visited many "commercial" hot spots on the base. Officer and Enlisted clubs were stocked with the best of steaks, shrimp, wine and whiskey, slot machines, and live entertainment imported from the United States, Australia, Taiwan, etc. These clubs were reported to have made large sums of money and after visiting one it was easy to see why.

Within a ten minute walk of the hospital was a Chinese restaurant, *Loom Foons*, affectionally known as the "Diarrhea Palace." If a group of ten people from our staff visited at one time you could predict with certainty that one or two would have explosive diarrhea for at least the next 24 to 48 hours. Occasionally a staff member was admitted to the hospital and given intravenous fluids for one or two days. Despite the occasional backlash, I visited *Loom Foons* at least once a month because it afforded the opportunity of leaving the hospital environment with a group of friends and enjoy a Chinese meal. An excellent meal could be had for under $4.00. I recall having my first real bird-nest soup at the restaurant; My friends laughed at me because bird feathers were all over my face from the pieces of the bird's nest boiled in the soup.

Other eating stops were available on Long Binh Post. Most of these were basically the same. For instance, the USARV Officers Club or the Military Police Officers Club had excellent food; a steak dinner with all the trimmings for $2.50 or lobster for $3.00, an array of entertainment including imported singers and bands, and slot machines. Each club generated huge revenues. I did not frequent many of theses clubs because of distance and lack of time.

Arthur Ashe, the tennis player, made a tour of Vietnam and I was able to break away for about an hour to watch him play tennis on a court near our hospital. The court was a simple, flat, level piece of ground with a net between two poles and white paint on the ground for the lines. No stands to sit in, fans just crowded around the court fence fighting for the best view.

Sometimes we provided the entertainment. One night one of the doctors who had just returned from months on a firebase got very drunk. He had acquired an AK-47 souvenir while at the firebase and had it out scaring everyone. It was decided he needed to be taught a lesson for such a prank. We waited until he passed out and was so deeply intoxicated that his reflexes at the elbow, knee, and ankle were markedly diminished. Dirt was then smudged on his uniform, his head and face were wrapped in bandages to mask his identity, outdated bank blood was splattered all over him, and then he was taken to the battle casualty admitting area of the hospital on a stretcher. It was a quiet night at 0200hrs and the personnel on duty treated him as a casualty and started an intravenous line. The neurosurgeon was called for an evaluation. Before he arrived, we had placed an X-ray on the bed of the head of a soldier who was admitted earlier and had died of a head injury. The neurosurgeon did an extensive neurology examination, looked at the X-ray, and declared our "patient" "expectant" [a term meaning the soldier was going to die within 24 hours with or without an operation]. Expectant soldiers were put behind a screened area and checked about every four hours. Our drunken doctor was put behind the expectant screen. After laughing for a long time, we went to bed. Hours later the doctor started to recover and was very surprised to find himself with an intravenous in his arm, a bloody bandage on his head, and an "expectant" sign at the bottom of his bed. He was not in a good mood for a couple of days but finally laughed with us. The neurosurgeon was not too happy we had gotten him out of bed but when he found out what we had done he laughed with us.

Almost every Quonset hut had at least one barbeque made from a fifty-gallon drum cut in half with a metal screen over the top to hold steak and shrimp. It was not uncommon to get a delivery of 100 steaks and 50 pounds of shrimp a week. Physicians working in the sexual transmission disease clinic would see Generals and Colonels with certain sexual contact maladies. These men wanted to be treated but did not want the episode entered in their health record. A deal was made: no record of venereal disease if food was provided to our hoochs on the weekend. We would divide up the goodies and either have a combined party or individual hooch parties. Before I left Vietnam I was tired of steaks and shrimp. Spaghetti and garlic bread became a real treat.

Casualties was sporadic and many scheduled parties had to be canceled at the last minute. Free nights were spent talking, getting catnaps, playing cards, or providing self-entertainment. Some had televisions and were privileged to watch the Army-Air Force channel. Almost everyone had some kind of radio to listen to the military radio station.

Free movies, with inexpensive buttered popcorn, were shown in the hospital compound about twice a week. The reel-to-reel projector jumped frames often, sometimes burned the film, and frequently broke down. Everyone harassed the poor projectionist. During one of my visits to the USAF compound at Tan Son Nhut, AFB, I had the marvelous experience of attending a real movie house. The USAF had built an air-conditioned, movie theatre complete with real popcorn poppers and melted butter. What a contrast! Our hospital personnel sitting under a tent flap on folding chairs in high humidity while the USAF personnel were viewing movies in an air-conditioned theater. Somehow it just did not seem fair.

Long Binh had shops selling clothes, furniture, Far East trinkets, haircuts, and assorted merchandise. The Army had a small PX nearby but rarely had anything good except toiletries. I purchased a hand carved table from an export shop. The table was carved in Hong Kong and shipped directly to the United States. Haircuts, at a cost of forty to sixty cents, were obtained from Vietnamese civilians in small shops dotting the post.

Near the conclusion of a hooch party, one of the doctors got a little too drunk. He stupidly dressed in the night attire of a Viet Cong sapper [enemy soldier that came under the wire at night and tried to blow up buildings and the ammunition dump]. With his face smeared black he proceeded to sneak down to the Commander's hooch and made a big commotion by tossing rocks on the tin roof. The Commander burst out the door, a loaded weapon in hand, and would have shot the doctor if he had seen him. The doctor got away with a prank that could have easily gotten him killed or in a lot of trouble if he had been found out.

One night the local bridge "club" in my hooch was missing a fourth so I reluctantly agreed to play one game. I had never played bridge before but I was pretty good at hearts and Rook®. A short course on how to bid and play ensued prior to dealing the cards. I had no idea how to bid but I knew my first hand was remarkable. I kept bidding, my partner thinking I was crazy. Finally, I won the bid well over what anyone thought was reasonable. I ended up bidding the highest in what I think was called no-trump and proceeded to take every trick. I found out I had accomplished a rare feat in bridge - A Grand Slam. No one of course believed I had never played bridge before; they even accused me of being a "sand bagger" or a "hustler". I left the table and told them we agreed to one hand and this couldn't get any better. They begged me to stay to be buried by their great skills. I never played bridge again.

Letters from home were always the highlight of the day. Mail call occurred seven days a week. Zoe Leone mailed a letter everyday and, when possible, I would write everyday, even when I was too tired to move. Sometimes I would fall asleep with pen in hand, waking to an unfinished letter with a line going off the page. Hearing from your sweetheart was always a great thrill. Zoe Leone's letters were always encouraging, full of love, talked of events of her day with the four children, opened feelings, and expressed all the things two people in love share. News of extended family happenings was also fun. My letters were filled with much of the same thing: work, being tired, loneliness, anticipation of coming home, meeting for Rest and Recreation in Hawaii, or experiences of the day. I saved many of her letters to re-read on days no letter arrived. It was comforting and relaxing to put on some great classical music and sit in my room and re-read her letters. Mailing letters from Vietnam was easy, simply put the letter in an addressed envelope, write FREE on the upper right hand corner of the envelope and post it.

Before leaving for Vietnam I took a couple of weeks to get the family settled in Cedar City, Utah. Cedar City had a weekly newspaper: The Iron County Record, which I made sure Zoe Leone subscribed to. During the two weeks stay in Cedar City before going to Vietnam, I went to the Iron Country Record office and arranged to have an advertisement placed in the newspaper at Christmas time. Just before Christmas, I wrote a letter and asked Zoe Leone if she had seen the ad in the newspaper. By coincidence my letter and the newspaper containing the ad arrived on the same day. She opened the letter first, read about the ad, then quickly opened the newspaper and found the ad: *Merry Christmas To Zonie, Mason, Yvonne, Kendall, Valerie, From Dad in Vietnam.* Zoe Leone cried all day long. Loneliness, love, and happiness combined to make a great memory that has lasted a lifetime.

A short distance down the road from the hospital was an Olympic sized swimming pool constructed of plastic and wood. It was about three feet deep and the only pool of such size on Long Binh. Only twice did I get a chance to swim but I do recall it was fun and relaxing.

Being able to attend weekly church service was always a boost, when I could go. The Church of Jesus Christ of Latter-day Saint [LDS] Chaplain had arranged to hold the Sunday meetings, sacrament and priesthood, in the main auditorium of USARV headquarters. The room was spacious, air-conditioned, had comfortable seats, and provided a luxury we did not anticipate. Being together in a war zone with men in uniform of the same faith is an experience of great spiritual strength.

On one occasion the LDS Chaplains made arrangements to have a religious retreat for LDS members at Tan Son Nhut AFB near Saigon. Members on Long Binh and areas surrounding Tan Son Nhut AFB were bussed to the AFB Chapel. A General Authority of the Church of Jesus Christ of Latter-day Saints flew from the United States to tour Vietnam. The spacious AFB Chapel was filled with members from all three branches of the military who spent the day being spiritually uplifted, crying, laughing, and sharing experiences. A memory of closeness to God in a far away land stricken with the terrors and horrors of war. Words cannot express the exquisite oneness I felt with God the Father as I prayerfully requested His confirmation of the importance of my work and mission to others in Vietnam.

More than once a group from the hospital went to Saigon for the day. One visit was to the U.S. Army hospital in Saigon, the "showcase" for the military in Vietnam. Brightly waxed floors, clean sheets on stateside hospital beds, and spick and span operating rooms with mounted lights and all the trimmings. The Army had converted an old school building into a hospital. Great pains had been made to make the hospital look, feel, and smell like a first class stateside hospital. Doctors and nurses wore starched, clean, Class B uniforms and some nurses wore white uniforms. A regular elective surgery schedule was posted daily which included such surgeries as fixing slanted eyes and doing breast implants on the Vietnamese mistresses of high ranking U.S. military and civilian officials and, occasionally, the wives of high-ranking Vietnamese government officials. The hospital was an unreal world to step into in Vietnam and I was relieved to leave. Before returning home we had lunch on a boat restaurant moored at the Saigon river. The duck was excellent. Three to four days later the restaurant was blown up by the Viet Cong.

Saigon seemed to be a haven for high ranking American government officials [military and civilian] who thought they knew what was happening in the entire country from protected residences. Most lived in first class villas with air conditioning, a chauffeured car, sometimes a mistress, servants, and an active social life. Reflecting back on what I saw it is now easy to realize why the American people were fed false information and given a story line about the war which was self serving to these high officials of the United States government.

Out of Country

A physician from the 24th Evacuation Hospital was sometimes needed to accompany a wounded soldier being evacuated to Japan. A rotating list ensured that all physicians, regardless of rank, shared the opportunity to get out of Vietnam for three days: departure day, a shopping day in Tokyo, and day of return. I made two such trips to Japan. Any trip out-of-country required you to exchange your MPC's for U.S. dollars. Prior to boarding the outbound plane, you passed through a small room with a large garbage can labeled: Amnesty. Anyone having drugs, i.e. marijuana, heroin, morphine, could drop the drugs in the can without penalty.

When the physician's name was posted as going to Japan, all members of the 24th Evacuation Hospital, officers and enlisted, gave cash to the physician prior to departure for things to be purchased at the military PX in Japan. On my two trips I carried $3,000 to $4,000 and spent one-half of my time in Tokyo at the PX filling orders. The Army-Air Force PX system published a catalog featuring a wide range of items at very low prices. One could order directly from the catalog but it was not as convenient or amazing as walking into the PX with a wad of cash ready for frenzied buying. What fun! The PX was geared to shopping sprees and employees were assigned to the buyer in order to keep the items together, and help transport them to the Post Office [just outside the door] so they could be packaged for safe shipment. Items could be shipped directly to the United States or to Vietnam.

Our family was the recipient of china, tableware, stereos, and other miscellaneous items. I was broke most of the time saving money buying excellent "things" at low prices. What fun the family had unwrapping the large packages I sent home two months before departing Vietnam.

Riding the subway in Japan was an eye opener. Very crowded. At many stations, subway "packers" pushed people into the train so tightly you could not raise your arm from your side to scratch your nose!

A hot soaking bubble bath at the Sanyo Hotel [military hotel in Tokyo] was about as close to heaven as possible on earth. After the bath, an extremely tender Kobe steak tasted marvelous. On the evening of my first trip I boarded the subway and attended the opera, *Madame Butterfly*. The opera was sung in Italian. Being an American in a Japanese audience provided quite a contrast, and I loved it.

During my second trip to Japan I arranged a total of five days of temporary duty at the Osaka University Medical School to present lectures on *Anesthesia techniques in Trauma*. I had been invited by Dr. Onji, Professor and Chairman of the Department of Anesthesia, an anesthesiologist who did part of his training at the University of Utah. Dr. Carter Ballinger, Chairman of the Anesthesia Service at the University of Utah had connected us. After dropping off the wounded soldier and doing the required half-day PX "shopping", I boarded the famous bullet train from Tokyo to Osaka. Traveling at high speed in an air-conditioned train with all the luxuries and amenities was a real treat.

Dr. Onji invited me to stay at his home, a typical Japanese home with a very special Tea Ceremony room. When you entered the home you took off your shoes and replaced them with sandals. Dr. and Mrs. Onji greeted me in traditional Japanese clothes, reserved for special occasions. I slept on the floor of the Tea Ceremony room on a soft mattress with a block of wood as a pillow.

Mrs. Onji belonged to a local Tea Ceremony Club that had a goal to preserve the ancient ritual of the Japanese tea ceremony. The Tea Ceremony room was walled with bamboo and a section was set apart for cooking tea and preforming the ceremony. Mrs. Onji wanted me to see the Tea Ceremony even thought I did not drink tea. She dressed in a traditional Japanese Kimono and spent two hours fascinating me. Each movement in the ceremony is done with such grace and purposefulness. Easy to see and understand the great pleasure and peace of mind the Tea Ceremony provides you. Total concentration is required for each delicate movement. Thoughts of the outside world are obliterated as you watch with intent the steps of the Tea Ceremony. The attention to detail, the concentration required, the inner beauty of the movements was extraordinary; an experience I shall vividly remember. Hopefully the Tea Ceremony will remain a tradition in Japan for centuries to come.

After I presented a successful lecture at the University, Dr. Onji had a special treat for me. He had been working with the Japan Worlds Fair Committee in Osaka setting up emergency medical services. Because of his busy schedule he had not had the opportunity to visit the site of the World Fair and see the fruits of his service, even though he had been invited many times. He took me to the Worlds Fair where he was treated as a VIP and I was a tag along. We first toured the emergency medical service building, and then we were escorted throughout the World Fair in an ambulance. No walking for me! Each of the major pavilions, e.g. Russian, Canadian, United States, Japanese had prearranged a personal tour for Dr. Onji and me. We would pull up in the ambulance at the back door [no lines to wait in] where the pavilion director met us and toured us through the pavilion. What a wonderful opportunity afforded me! Circumstances and events just fell into place to allow me to see almost all the major sights of the World Fair in less than one day. Today I consider it a blessing in my life that I was able to visit with Dr. Onji and his family.

The highlight of out-of-country rest and recreation [R & R] was the one, mid-tour seven-day trip, provided by the military. Designated sites included Hong Kong, Singapore, Hawaii, and Australia. The military flew you to and from the site free of charge aboard charted airplanes. You paid for food, lodging, and entertainment. Of course the most popular site was Hawaii for two reasons: A touch of the United States and the opportunity to see loved ones. Some soldiers brought their families to Hawaii, others met their wife or sweetheart. The military allowed visits as far as Hawaii but not the mainland.

My R & R was in Hawaii. Zoe Leone flew from Cedar City and grandparents tended our four children. Unless you have had a long separation from a loved one you cannot feel or even imagine the intensity of anticipation of re-uniting for just a short time. Many military personnel must be separated from their loved ones, especially the Navy in peace time, but the circumstances of war, possible death or injury, and constant reminders imbedding the Vietnam war images, made the anxiety of separation more intense.

Zoe Leone had flown to Hawaii a day earlier and was waiting at the off-loading site at Fort Derussy, on Waikiki Beach. Reunion was a combination of crying and hugging mixed with joy, happiness, and love. We rented a car and stayed at a small motel near the Polynesian Culture Center on the northeast side of Oahu. The location was secluded and close to the Hawaiian Temple. Our days were filled with sleeping in late, eating "plate lunches", and enjoying the beach.

The Hawaiian Temple is one of the oldest temples of the Church of Jesus Christ of Latter Day Saints. The Hawaiian Temple is small, making the ambiance very personal. We had previously fallen in love with the Polynesian people so time inside the Temple and sharing spiritual experiences was sweet. R & R was a blessing to our marriage. We reviewed our children's lives and tried to formulate future plans. Spiritual and physical bonding provided us the opportunity to become one in the sight of God. Some soldiers found it hard, if not impossible, to return to Vietnam after R & R. I left R & R with a refreshed soul, with renewed faith in what

I was doing in Vietnam, and a strengthened testimony not only of God but also of my patriotism to the United States.

R & R was a Godsend for most soldiers. Civilians will never understand the stresses and sacrifices of war. Movies, books, music, and pictures do not capture the essence of heat, sweat, blood, smells, bugs, fear, or hate. There are no descriptive words to describe one of the most long-standing challenges to man: WAR.

CHAPTER 7

OUR ALLIES

THROUGH THE BACK DOOR OF my hooch were buildings housing some of the Thailand troops. When the wind was just right, the scent of Thai cooking drifted over. Curry seemed to be the dominant spice. You got the distinct impression that curry held the Thai's soul together, if not the soul, then at least the integrity of the bodies cells was dependent on a daily dose of curry. One Thai soldier I was going to give a general anesthetic to vomited just prior to the induction and deposited a conglomeration of curried rice all over my hands, shirt, pants, the floor, and the end of the operating table. His reflexes were intact so there was no danger of lung aspiration. The smell of rice mixed with curry and gastric juice was more than I could take. I had only been in-country for a few weeks and was not used to the putrid smell. I vomited into the kick bucket for the first and last time in Vietnam

The Commanding General of the Thailand Army in Vietnam allegedly stepped out of his private helicopter to review the troops with his sidearm on. Somehow his pistol discharged, shooting him in the foot! On arrival at our hospital he was not a happy man, especially when I told him he would have to have a spinal anesthetic because he had just eaten. He insisted on a general anesthetic but my medical judgment prevailed and he had a very successful spinal. Because of the nature of the injury, the General had to come back a second time for surgery. For the second surgery, I restricted everything by mouth for 12 hours and honored the General's request for a general anesthetic. On his departure day, everyone who had rendered care to the General was ordered to his bedside. Each of us was given a gift of appreciation. I received a silver cigarette case, which I displayed with pride for years, and eventually gave to my son Kendall as a memento of my Vietnam experience. When I went to Thailand thirty-five years later, it was impossible to locate the General to repeat a thank you.

Dr. Buu, a South Vietnamese Army physician, was sent to the 24th Evacuation Hospital by U.S. Army headquarters in Saigon for six weeks of On-the-Job Training [OJT] in anesthesia. Dr. Buu had a limited English vocabulary so the Vietnamese Government sent Sergeant Saun as his interpreter. On the day the pair arrived I gave them a tour of the operating rooms and discovered Dr. Buu had only a rudimentary knowledge of anesthesia. His medical education was dismal and I soon determined that Dr. Buu's anesthesia training was going to be difficult.

I oriented Dr. Buu in operating room procedures, gave him didactic lectures twice a day, and assigned written homework. Eventually the "team" of Dr. Buu and the Sergeant Saun were allowed to do cases in the operating room under very close supervision. During lulls in casualties, the "team" administered anesthesia to soldiers coming back for re-exploration or secondary closure. Dr. Buu was never allowed to administer an anesthetic without continuous direct supervision by one of our anesthesia staff. In 1969 the main "workhorse anesthetic" was halothane. As an anesthesia team, we decided to teach Dr. Buu how to administer halothane anesthesia despite the fact that ether was the main anesthetic used in the Vietnamese Army Hospital in Saigon. Sergeant Saun turned out to be bright and learned much faster than Dr. Buu. Sergeant Saun ended up being our conduit to teach Dr. Buu how to administer anesthesia. Dr. Buu was quiet, cordial, and pleasant but he was not cut out to be an anesthesiologist. The Buu and Saun "team" could give a halothane anesthetic when the soldier was healthy and there was no deviation from the norm.

Sergeant Saun was an interesting character that reminded me of the scrounger in the movie, *King Rat*. He was always making deals to sell air conditioners, cigarettes, and wild nights in Saigon. A group from the hospital went to Saigon with the Sergeant for the day and found out he had a family to support and was scrounging to make ends meet. I liked the Sergeant and wished he could have been assigned to the 24th Evacuation

Hospital. Perhaps our influence and his intelligence could have been the elements to get him into the South Vietnamese medical school.

When Dr. Buu and Sergeant Saun left they gave me a lovely shell picture of a Vietnam scene still displayed on our living room wall. Everyone in anesthesia enjoyed teaching Dr. Buu the fundamentals of anesthesia. We knew that when he left the 24th Evacuation Hospital he would be considered the "expert" trained by the Americans. Considerable efforts were made to teach Dr. Buu to be as safe and competent as possible in a very limited training window. What happened after Dr. Buu and Sergeant left has remained unknown. Perhaps Dr. Buu was able to obtain further training in anesthesia. We only hope our efforts to train Dr. Buu made an impact on the quality of anesthesia care in Vietnam.

Occasionally members of our surgical and anesthesia teams traveled as a group to Conghoa Hospital, the biggest and best South Vietnamese Army hospital in Saigon. The hospital was old but was kept clean and functional, despite lack of funds and a long-lasting war. Patient care was a family affair. Family members brought food, provided bedside care, and slept on the floor alongside the patient's bed during the night.

Every Vietnamese physician had a thirty-year service obligation in the Army. The Vietnamese government allowed physicians to run a private clinic in the early morning and late evening in order to supplement their meager military income. Surgery at Conghoa hospital was scheduled from 0900hrs-1300hrs, and then again from 1530hrs to 1700hrs; the time from 1300hrs to 1530hrs being a "siesta" time. The restricted surgery schedule kept pace with fresh casualties but secondary closures and reparative work was almost non-existent. These limited surgical hours meant many casualties would lie bleeding on stretchers in front of the hospital all night waiting for 0900hrs and the arrival of the doctors and nurses.

Our orthopedic surgeons called the orthopedic wards at the Conghoa hospital an "orthopedic museum". Severe complications seen on the wards were only depicted in outdated medical textbooks. These severe orthopedic complications were the result of inappropriate initial surgery and the lack of follow-up surgery. Grotesque disfigurements of limbs, and hands were not uncommon. Our orthopedic surgeons recommended more than once to the Vietnamese surgeons to send all the complicated cases on the wards home [nothing could be done for them] and to concentrate on spending more time on the initial surgery and provide time for proper follow-up surgery. Trying to take care of chronic orthopedic complications had definitely become a fruitless endeavor.

Anesthesia at the Conghoa hospital was not the best. The Chief anesthesiologist had trained in France for one year. He had established a six-week course to train nurses to give anesthesia. After completing the six-week course the nurses were sent to small villages or military assignments. I tried to teach in the operating rooms during my visits but it didn't make much of a lasting impression because of time restraints.

Anesthesia equipment at Conghoa hospital was a conglomeration of donated U.S. Military Anesthesia Machines, a few dilapidated foreign machines, and donated ventilators. Ether was the primary anesthetic agent. Blood was a scarce commodity. One of my frustrations was to enter an operating room and be shown an anesthetic record that was piece of art work; "railroad tracks" for the blood pressure, a stable heart rate, and non-changing vital signs despite the fact that blood was hanging and dripping in at a very, very slow rate. I was told, "Everything is fine". On more than one occasion I was allowed to take the blood pressure and found it very low, certainly not a reflection of the "railroad tracks" on the anesthetic record. My reaction was to demand more blood, use a blood pump to push in about three to five units and watch the blood pressure rapidly come back to normal, the heart rate slow, and the Vietnamese anesthesia team dazzled at the chain of events.

During one of the trips to Saigon, I visited the University of South Vietnam Medical School with Dr. Buu and Sergeant Saun. The medical library had a limited choice of journals and medical books, certainly not enough to meet the needs of medical students. In 1995 a Vietnamese student at the Uniformed Services University of the Health Sciences in Bethesda, MD, returned to his homeland for a visit and I gave him one of my books, *The Anesthesia Machine*, to donate to the library. He came back with a picture of himself presenting the book to the President of the medical school. It made me feel good to be able to make a small but meaningful contribution. If I ever get the opportunity to travel back to Saigon I will make sure I take some up-to-date anesthesia books to donate to the library.

Passing Vietnamese Army posts on the way to Saigon allowed me to see the inadequate housing provided for the soldiers and their families.

Morale in the Vietnamese Army was not high in 1969 and 1970. American soldiers said the Vietnamese troops would call in American troops to do the risky work and then, if we were successful, the Vietnamese would go in for the "cleanup" and claim victory. It must be remembered, war to the Vietnamese was a way of life. Vietnam had been at war for years, to them we were just another foreign army tramping in the steps of the "liberators" of the past. Why should the South Vietnamese be overly excited to fight, fight, and fight knowing the leadership at the highest level in the South Vietnamese government was dishonest, corrupt, and incompetent? A puppet government held together by the "glue" of American money.

Vietnamese ingenuity made up for some abject poverty. One good example of such ingenuity were the "tin-can" houses on the road to Saigon. Beer and soda cans were separated at the seams, pounded flat, two sides bent back a short distance so the flattened cans could be interlinked, and then connected to form long "building panels". Panels were made into walls and roofs. The "tin-can house" was effective in keeping out the sun and rain.

The efforts of the United States in helping the South Vietnamese to avoid communism seems useless in retrospect. The few Vietnamese who came to the United States were rewarded with a taste of democracy. The South Vietnamese Army was betrayed by their despot political leaders. When Americans left the soil of South Vietnam in the final helicopter, the "glue-money" was gone, and the South Vietnamese government came tumbling down.

CHAPTER 8

THE ENEMY

N EXT DOOR TO THE MAIN complex of Quonset huts comprising the 24th Evacuation Hospital was a designated Prisoner of War [POW] hospital. The Commander of the 24th Evacuation Hospital was responsible for 1) the care of wounded POWs, 2) the security of the POW hospital, and 3) enforcing the Geneva Convention rules applied to wounded POWs. A fence, topped with barbed wire, surrounded the POW hospital compound and guard towers were positioned at each corner of the rectangular structure.

Entrance to the POW hospital required a security clearance issued by the Commander. For instance, physicians and nurses assigned to the Walter Reed Army Institute of Research, housed at the 24th Evacuation Hospital, were not allowed to enter the POW hospital. The Geneva convention had a strict rule against any research on POWs and this rule was strictly adhered to by the U.S. Army. I was cleared to enter the POW hospital and ended up doing most of the anesthesia. My introduction to the POW hospital was a bit of a shock. The Commander of the 24th Evacuation hospital had allegedly been a tank driver in World War II prior to becoming a physician. During my first week in Vietnam I was "invited" by the Colonel to accompany him on morning rounds at the POW hospital. I arrived at his office at the appointed time to find him with a swagger stick under his left arm, starched uniform, and polished shoes; a bit out of place for the 24th Evacuation Hospital to say the least. We proceeded to the hospital where the guards came to attention and saluted as the Colonel and I entered. The individual POWs were called to "attention" and those that could stand were required to place both big toes against a white line painted on the floor in front of the row of hospital beds. The Colonel proceeded to "inspect" the standing POWs. He put the end of the swagger stick next to their nose and asked how they were feeling. The Colonel was very rigid but did not abuse any patient in my presence, nor were there any rumors of such. I think his methods were a way of letting the POWs know who was in charge, that they were POWs despite being patients in a hospital, and that they could expect good care. An eye-opening opportunity for me and not one that many anesthesiologists have experienced. I was happy to get back to work after the orientation visit.

All POWs had access to the same care as U.S. soldiers. The POW hospital had one operating room. The initial surgical procedure on POW's was done in the main operating rooms of the 24th Evacuation Hospital and follow up surgeries were usually preformed in the POW hospital operating room. POWs were always treated with respect. Our physicians honored the Hippocratic Oath: giving care to all, irrespective of race, circumstances, or the fact the POWs were the enemy. When a POW was discharged from the POW hospital, he was turned over to the interrogation unit of the Armed Forces of the South Vietnamese Army. One of my saddest memories of Vietnam was the return of a few POWs after being interrogated by the South Vietnamese Army. It was alleged the interrogators slogan for captured prisoners was: "If they are innocent, beat them until they are guilty." Interrogation was sometimes so brutal the POWs were returned to the 24th Evacuation for reparative surgery.

Giving anesthesia in the POW hospital was a unique experience. It was here I learned of the intense propaganda against Americans taught to the North Vietnamese Army (NVA) and Viet Cong soldiers. Intense fear on the face of a POW was common as an intravenous line was started. I will never forget the wild look on the eyes of the young POW who spit on me as I was trying to render medical care. Defiance, dedication, and determination burned in the eyes of the Viet Cong and NVA POW's. This was totally the opposite of what was being said about the enemy on Army TV, in *Stripes* [an Army publication], on the Army radio, and in publications from home. Without doubt, these enemy soldiers were determined to win the war, no matter how long it took and despite the cost. An enemy determined to die rather than return to what they perceived as slavery and dominance by foreigners. Many prior conquers, Chinese, French, and Japanese, had imbedded a desire in the soldiers to rid the country of any foreign influence.

Sometimes just putting on the blood pressure cuff was perceived as a life-threatening experience by a POW. One day I was fortunate enough to have an interpreter present and asked through him why a 17-year-old POW was so terrified. The POW had been told the Americans would kill him in the POW hospital and he was absolutely certain I was the one designated to kill him! POWs who required two or three operations became somewhat trusting over time.

For a short time, we had an NVA "physician" as a POW patient. He spoke broken English and came to the operating room with me. His presence was very helpful in explaining to the POWs that I was not going to hurt them but was going to give them an anesthetic for their operation. His presence made a world of difference in the POWs attitude. We gave the POWs care equal to American soldiers but I doubt the POWs had the capacity or background to fully appreciate our efforts.

Occasionally a regional anesthetic was the anesthetic of choice for the POW's surgery. The axillary block proved to be particularly effective with certain modifications of the technique in POWs. To preform an axillary block in an American soldier a very small needle [25ga] was inserted high in the armpit. When a paresthesia [a shooting pain like you feel when you bump your elbow] to the hand occurred the needle was positioned in the right place to inject the local anesthetic. In the arm pit the three nerves (median, ulna, radial), the axillary artery, and the axillary vein are wrapped up in a tubular sheath [like Saran Wrap®]. Placement of the needle inside the sheath results in a successful nerve block 96% of the time. Preforming the block on American soldiers was easy because they could tell you when the needle touched a nerve (paresthesia). Doing the block on a POW was next to impossible using the paresthesia technique because you could not tell if the POW was feeling pain from the needle in the armpit or just pain from the needle. It was necessary to alter the axillary block technique. The pulse of the axillary artery was palpated with the index finger and held stable. The needle was then advanced over the middle of the tip of the index fingernail into the artery, carefully withdrawing blood as the needle entered the artery. Once you enter the artery, you continue to withdraw or advance the needle very slowly and carefully until the blood return stops. The tip of the needle now lies outside the artery but still inside the tubular sheath. Injection of small incremental doses of local anesthetic, with frequent aspirations to make sure the needle tip has not inadvertently re-entered the artery resulted in a block of the three nerves to the lower arm. The POWs watched the axillary block and it was pleasing to see the amazement on their faces as their arm became numb. After the surgery the POW would have pain relief until the body absorbed the local anesthetic.

One unfortunate medical incident occurred involving an older [about 65] woman, an alleged Viet Cong sympathizer, who was brought to the POW hospital for care. She had been carrying military supplies on her bicycle down the Ho Chi Minh trail from North Vietnam to South Vietnam. Somewhere adjacent the to 24th Evacuation Hospital, she had encountered a land mine that resulted in a deep wound to the femur. The NVA's medical team treated her initially. Bleeding was stopped, maggots were placed in the wound, and the wound was wrapped with a sterile bandage. Years ago, before antibiotics, maggots had been used successfully to treat wound infections in the United States. Maggots eat only dead tissue and leave living tissue. During her initial assessment at the 24th Evacuation the wound was found to be glistening clean and free of infection. Unfortunately, a "hot-shot" surgeon happened to be assigned the case and felt penicillin therapy was required. He prescribed a very large dose of penicillin-VK, a particular form of penicillin which has a potassium molecule attached to each penicillin moiety. The cumulative dose of potassium proved toxic and she had a cardiac arrest from which she could not be resuscitated. The case was reviewed in the hospital's monthly morbidity and mortality meeting and the physician was placed on probation. He was later involved in other mishaps and had to be relieved of duty as a surgeon in Vietnam.

The Viet Cong had detailed maps of Long Binh and the 24th Evacuation Hospital. Many ambulatory POWs would embark the helicopter, walk directly to the door of the receiving area, and then down the corridor to the POW hospital. Many Viet Cong sympathizers worked as civilians on base; occasionally one of them could be seen "walking off the distance" between buildings to make maps.

I considered working in the POW hospital as a special privilege. I learned a great deal about humanity, experienced things that changed my opinion of the "enemy", and ended up a better man because of the POW exposure.

After the war ended the tragedies of battle on the North Vietnamese and South Vietnamese were released. Over 3,500,000 Vietnamese, including the Army of the Republic of Vietnam, served during the "American War". Of these, 300,000 are still missing, 440,000 North Vietnamese are dead, and 220,000 South Vietnamese are dead. Hundreds of thousands of military and civilians were disabled during the war. Post Traumatic Stress Disorder was seen in both friendly and enemy troops, as well as civilians on both sides.

Viet Cong and North Vietnamese soldiers were tenacious, experienced, and well trained. The French left Vietnam in defeat and characterized the Vietnam People's Army as one of the best combat infantry forces in the world. The determination of the enemy to win the Vietnam War was grossly underestimated by the United States military and, especially, United States political leaders. Ho Chi Minh was certainly correct in July 1962 when he said: "It may perhaps take ten years to do it, but our heroic compatriots in the South will defeat them in the end. I think the Americans greatly underestimate the determination of the Vietnamese people." Americans did not have the patience and staying power to fight a long protracted war. Americans expected the Vietnam War to be like fast food, a quick and decisive victory. As the Vietnam War played out, with promise after promise of early victory, the American people lost resolve, and many became complacence or expressed anti-war sentiments. The citizens of North Vietnam were mobilized to be the eyes and ears of the army. As Ho Chi Minh said of the citizens in North Vietnam: ...*they feed and keep the soldiers...they constitute an inexhaustible source of strength for the army.* The enemy, soldiers and civilians, were characterized as a bundle of chopsticks; bound together they are very difficult to break but easy to break one by one. Eventually the determination and holding power of the North Vietnamese and Viet Cong won out as Americans left Vietnam by order of the President of the United States.

CHAPTER 9

IMPRESSIONS

WHY DID I GO TO Vietnam? Of course the most compelling reason was the set of orders in my hand from the U.S. Army to serve one year in Vietnam. My exposure to the Vietnam War had been skewed, limited, and propagandized. With orders in hand it was a time to reflect on the war because I knew it was important to go for the right reasons in order to maintain sanity, morals, and love of country.

In 1968 the U.S. suffered a psychological defeat at the hands of the enemy. North Vietnamese and Viet Cong opened the ground attack phase of Tet in cities and towns throughout South Vietnam. Many South Vietnamese soldiers were home on leave because of the Tet holiday. The Viet Cong drive was beaten back in most places but at the cost of more than 1,700 American lives and twice that number in the Army of the Republic of Vietnam (ARVN).

By 1969, anti-Vietnam War sentiment had entered the open opposition phase in the United States. More and more citizens, including those in military uniform, were asking poignant questions about the war. A flak jacket and steel pot do not blind American soldiers to anti-war sentiment. As a physician, wounded soldiers evacuated from Vietnam to Brooke Army Medical Center in San Antonio were constantly bombarding me with confusing questions of why America was defending South Vietnam. The official military propaganda line during my residency training at Brooke Army Medical Center was "Fight communism and keep the world free of tyranny." However, American journalists reporting from Vietnam in newspapers and magazines were presenting what appeared to be a valid point of view that America did not have succinct reasons to be in Vietnam. The President and Congress resorted to platitudes and generalities to support the ever-growing American presence in Vietnam. America's long-term goals seemed vague.

Soldiers do not get to chose their war. Whatever is happening and wherever it is happening, soldiers are ordered to go and they go. National leaders eventually pay the price for bad decisions, especially decisions leading to needless deaths. Hitler and Stalin were power-crazed men in World War II who paid with the price of insanity. Both men gained power by stepping through the puddles of other men's blood. Any man who bombards rational thinking with carnage cannot evade the eventual deterioration of the brain; deterioration which will lead to heinous acts and mental imbalance. A war is something judged in the eyes of many. Good, bad, evil, moral - your perception depends on which side you are on and the eventual outcome. Perhaps passion and longings of youth to participate in war is a factor. Looking back at my present age of 77 and it is difficult to recall the forceful youthful passions quelled by the humdrum concerns of adulthood. My guileless conviction in high school was that America was always right because democracy had been established by God in America. How little did I know about how far national leaders would go to protect self-interests and political life? After only a few months in Vietnam, I separated my belief of God establishing America's democracy (I still believe this) from the false notion of America always being right. My background had prepared me to accept orders for war despite unclear reasons. The President, the elected Congress, and the majority of United States citizens seemed to be in support of the conflict when I left for Vietnam.

Serving in the military as a medical officer was a blessing. At the end of medical school, just a week prior to graduation, our class took the Oath of Hippocrates. I read the Oath many times during my internship and residency and knew it was my duty as a physician to go where I was needed. My military uniform pointed me to the battlefield where young men stood in harms way to preserve concepts of freedom, democracy, and liberty. Despite open criticism of the Vietnam War, soldiers were in Vietnam and needed medical support. Patriotism was another factor compelling me to serve. No, I did not want to leave my wife and four children, but orders required me to fulfill my responsibilities. I put any doubts about the war behind me, concentrated entirely on serving wounded soldiers and my country, and boarded the plane to Vietnam.

Before receiving orders for Vietnam my officer designation changed from Reserve to Regular Army. My internship and anesthesia residency training in the Army required pay back time so it was expedient for the Army to make the designated change. Regular Army designation had few advantages at the time and many disadvantages. As Regular Army, when assignments came, you went. Physicians trained in civilian programs at the time were drafted for two years as Reserve Army officers. The Army offered them a deal: voluntarily sign up for three years and be assured of not serving in Vietnam. Many accepted the bribe, markedly increasing my chances of serving in Vietnam. When I arrived in Vietnam I found many Reserve Army physicians who had turned down the "bargain"; some were happy with their lot, others bitter.

Young men and women must realize military assignments are not always based on what you know and how well qualified you are, but on who you know and how well you can work the system. Point: father or mother is a senator or congressman—Avoid Vietnam. Point: Escape to college: Avoid Vietnam. Point: Graduate from an illustrious name University-Avoid Vietnam. Point: Be a working class young man living in the inner city or in a small town-Orders for Vietnam almost without fail.

On arrival in Vietnam I was full of enthusiasm to serve. My light was soon dimmed as I became a victim of cynicism. America was in an upheaval over the war. Soldiers were being spit on at home. American soldiers were called "baby killers," "monsters," "war mongers," when they returned to their home towns, the same home towns where crowds met returning soldiers of World War II and Korea at the train station with bands and banners. Now the Vietnam veteran, at best, was met at the train station by his immediate family, most of whom avoided the subject of Vietnam. Families were grateful to have their son or daughter return alive but not willing to let them pour out their heart about what they had experienced in Vietnam. Despite extensive reading about the Vietnam War prior to my assignment, I was naive. Nothing prepared me for the psychological impact of the war. Written words, war movies, and personal testimonies failed to prepare me for the fear, unfairness, carnage, ruination of lives, wetness and smell of blood, stench of open intestines hanging down the legs and on the chest, and the sound of constant crying of the wounded until anesthesia provided welcome pain relief and disappearance from the war for a short time.

Constant exposure to carnage changed me. Did I get used to the blood baths, disfigurement, and ruined lives of soldiers? No. A hole was left in my heart. I did build up a barrier of acceptance, "it was my duty." Work, work, work, saved me from having to intellectually confront the dichotomy of the Vietnam War. Not until years later did I have to face the consequences of pent up emotions successfully avoided in Vietnam.

New perspectives of life values were formed. I leaned on my strong religious background. I questioned the stupidity of war but recognized the frailties of man since the beginning of life on earth. Despite obvious lying by the leaders of America, I retained love for the Constitution and the foundation of freedom in the United States. Love for Zoe Leone and the children markedly increased as I observed the destruction of marriages from death and adultery. Love increased immensely for the dead and wounded soldiers and for my peers caring for the wounded. After returning home, I noticed a much deeper and profound love for nature; sunsets, flowers, animals, ocean waves, etc., were transformed to a higher level of appreciation.

The inundating carnage I observed penetrated my protective mental barriers, upsetting my intellect no differently than an infecting rabies virus would do. Each central nervous system cell seemed to be penetrated by something sinister but indescribable. I knew men commonly denounced God in war. Now I was faced with seeing needless death and destruction. I was reminded of two passages from the *Book of Mormon* describing the useless carnage of war:

> _Ether 14:21-23_ And so great and lasting had been the war, and
> so long had been the scene of bloodshed and carnage,
> that the whole face of the land was covered with the
> bodies of the dead. And so swift and speedy was the
> war that there was none left to bury the dead, but they
> did march forth from the shedding of blood, leaving the

bodies of both men, women, and children strewed upon the face of the land, to become a prey to the worms of the flesh. And the scent thereof went forth upon the face of the land, even upon all the face of the land; wherefore the people became troubled by day and by night, because of the scent thereof.

Ether 15:16,19,20,22 And it came to pass that when it was night they were weary and retired to their camps; and after they had retired to their camps they took up a howling and a lamentation for the loss of the slain of their people; and so great were their cries, their howling's and lamentations, that they did rend the air exceedingly. And behold, the Spirit of the Lord had ceased striving with them, and Satan had full power over the hearts of the people; for they were given up unto the hardness of their hearts, and the blindness of their minds that they might be destroyed; wherefore they went again to battle. And it came to pass that they fought all that day, and when the night came they slept upon their swords. And when the night came they were drunken with anger, even as a man who is drunken with wine; and they slept again upon their swords.

One of the strongest deterrents to loss of testimony in God was the gratitude still in my heart as I watched wounded men made better and sent home. To hold their hand and say, *well done, we love you,* was comforting to me. Knowing I was there to help in my small way and being a part of a fine tuned professional team, rendering the best trauma care in the world was uplifting. Yet it was always difficult to leave the "safe haven" of my hooch and return to the smells, sights, and sounds of the Vietnam War in the operating room. Never did I lose vision of who I was, why I was in Vietnam, and knowing my life would be changed forever.

My relationship with God the Father had a definite re-arrangement. Nothing could have prepared my mind for the upheaval of pre-formed ideas of the war. Philosophy and religion had been something I had intellectualized for years. My naive views were, I thought, pretty well set and thought out. But the intensified reality of war shakes up all your values like a washing machine. During the Vietnam War and immediately after, I had to re-think what life was really all about. Things that seemed to have value before the war became meaningless afterward. Never throughout the entire turmoil did I lose my testimony of God; in fact, my testimony is what sustained me. Every moral value, every personal belief, every commitment, and every goal was inspected closely, revised, and stored in superficial compartments of my mind so I could recall and revise again. My intellectual foundation was shaken. I recognized how easy it was for a soldier to forget God, seek other outlets for solace, and return embittered, disillusioned, and angry.

As a Mormon I had the opportunity to repeatedly participate in a very significant religious experience in the Temple. The Temple, as the House of the Lord, is the one place on earth where you can almost touch God. The Temple covenants entered into with our Father in Heaven encourage Mormons to live life on a high spiritual plane. From going to the Temple often before Vietnam, I knew the ultimate destiny and worth of Man. Man was not perceived as degraded, immoral, or as killing and maiming for pleasure. Man was created, pure, intelligent, a literal Son of God. Such a concept kept my soul glue intact and helped me weather the storm of visual, tactile, and olfactory abuse.

The Vietnam War was responsible for changing me from a simple, honest, questioning of ideas and events person, to one who was skeptical and sometimes cynical. Trust in others disappeared in the barrage of lies from American government officials, journalists, military leaders, and others I previously thought had the best interests of the country at heart instead of their personal gain.

Contrast the soldiers who died in the Vietnam War with the turncoats who refused to face responsibility and fled to Canada or elsewhere. Only the word coward can amply describe my feelings toward them. The ultimate slap in the face to democracy is to run from responsibility. I have always been taught that democracy is the most difficult form of government to keep alive. Running from responsibility is not acceptable to me. Many of those who died in previous wars and the living veterans today would label those who ran as cowards. Should they be forgiven for their weakness to face responsibility? Covering up an act of cowardice by intellectual rationalization does not justify the means. Those who ran will someday regret their departure despite the unfortunate amnesty issued by the United States government.

Most American soldiers were not the kind of young men to whom it would have occurred to get a teaching job or to go to divinity school in order to avoid the draft, or to get a logistical or noncombat intelligence job to avoid combat. Many were fresh out of high school, or just off the farm, or, the production line and came from a small town. I was impressed with a sign found over the door of a Marine Division Information Office that read: *For those who have fought for it, life has a special flavor the protected will never know.*

Many would ask, how can a doctor really know what the grunt [slang name for the soldier] felt in the bush? In total reality, no one can know the feelings of the grunt. No, I was not in the bush. The bush came to me via the mud on combat boots, the punji sticks embedded in feet and lower legs, the jungle clinging to open wounds, the stick used to tighten makeshift tourniquets around leg stumps, the maggots in some wounds of the enemy, the look of terror in the eyes of the soldier with his leg and arm blown off by a Viet Cong booby trap, and the multiple war experiences related by the wounded soldiers. Oneness with each other, grunt-physician-nurse, was solidified as you experienced the courage displayed by wounded soldiers who came to the hospital with limbs in shreds or missing altogether, faces in pieces, holes ripped in their heads with open exposure to their brain where their fears, their loves, their joys, their memories, and their hope for a future, both here and with their God, were stored. Those soldiers who were capable expressed heartfelt thanks for our help in saving their lives; a gratefulness that sustained many of us separated from our families, the country we loved, and our "normal" lives.

An extremely low point of morale for me in the war was the visit of Jane Fonda to North Vietnam. It seemed to me she was siding with the enemy as a ploy to get celebrity attention at home. She visited a number of establishments in Hanoi including the infamous "Hanoi Hilton" where American prisoners of war were housed. What was happening inside her head was beyond belief. For most of us she was aiding and abetting the enemy. Since when does being a celebrity qualify anyone to speak for soldiers fighting a war? What a slap in the face to all of us living and working in South Vietnam. Records of the America's Prisoners of War in Hanoi relate how devastating Ms. Fonda's visit was, both to morale and treatment. Ms. Fonda should have first gotten a taste of war before she made such a stupid mistake. Why didn't she volunteer for the infantry or as a field journalist? Then she could have walked on night patrol in the jungle and experienced the humidity, insects, darkness, and fear of eminent death at any moment. Or even better, let her crawl through a Viet Cong tunnel filled with booby traps, false endings, snakes, and perhaps at the end of the tunnel an AK-47 barrel stuck in her face. We would have loved to have her visit the 24th Evacuation Hospital and work side by side with us for one week. Any of these experiences would have imbedded her thoughts with the realities of war. Jane Fonda was not only naive, but she was duped by the North Vietnamese.

Think how excited we were to find out Mrs. Nixon was going to visit us. Here was a mother, a woman, someone who could grasp the senselessness of war. Perhaps she would be a spokesperson for the terrible maiming of the children of America's mothers. However, military officials made sure her visit was properly sanitized. The day before she arrived the nurses at the 24th Evacuation Hospital were given white uniforms, wards were cleaned to perfection, and everyone was put on best behavior. On the morning of her visit, all casts were covered with fresh white plaster, all wounded soldiers were given clean, starched, pajamas and bath robes, nurses were clothed in white uniforms, and anyone seeing Mrs. Nixon was required to be in a Class B uniform.

Mrs. Nixon arrived with an entourage you would not believe. Secret service agents and soldiers surrounded the hospital, armed with M-16s. Mrs. Nixon graciously followed her hospital "tour guide" through the sterile wards. She saw happy soldiers with gleaming white casts on legs and arms, clean beds, smiling nurses and doctors, just like at Walter Reed Hospital in Washington, D.C., and I'm sure she left with the impression that war was not as bad as it had been made out to be.

Tears were flowing down my face as I realized this sensitive woman was going to leave with a totally inaccurate impression of the Vietnam War carnage. I wanted to reach out, grab her, and take her to see the patients in the neurosurgical ICU who would be comatose for the rest of their lives, take her to see the soldiers missing arms and legs who had been moved to an adjacent closed ward the night before her visit, take her to see the near-dead soldiers in the surgical ICU being kept alive by ventilators and dedicated medical personnel, take her into the operating room to observe the blood on the floor, the smell emanating from the open bullet holes of intestines, and let her carry out the amputated mutilated leg of a soldier who had stepped on a land mine. Let her sit down with the loving nurses and Red Cross volunteers who listened to the emotional outcries of wounded soldiers, read letters from loved ones to soldiers missing eyes and write letters for soldiers who had no eyes or hands to hold the pen. Then Mrs. Nixon would have known why war has always been described as A LIVING HELL.

Mrs. Nixon was only one of many who received the "sanitized tour." The 24th Evacuation Hospital was the most active combat hospital nearest to Tan Son Nhut AFB so it was the site for visits by Senators, Congressmen, and celebrities. Only once did I see a Senator break out of the "sanitized tour," walk over to the door of the ICU and see what war was really like. I happened to be passing by when he made this courageous move. The way I remember it was the officer in charge of the tour stood in front of the door and told the Senator he really did not want to go in the ICU. He made some lame excuse that the nurses were not prepared for such an unexpected visit. The Senator was kind and said he had been told he could visit any ward in the hospital. He politely asked the officer to step aside, and opened the door himself. I have always wanted to know what the Senator's impression was and to shake his hand for displaying such courage in the face of "military control."

My opinion then and now is that America's leaders need to see the results of their decisions on the personal lives of soldiers. If a leader never sends a son or daughter to war, how can they share the agony felt by parents all over America. When you make a decision and are not required to be responsible for the consequences, it becomes easier to make more bad decisions. Thank God, most of our military leaders know the consequences of sending young men and women into battle. Too bad every Senator and Congressman is not required, during a war, to spend two weeks carrying the backpack for a grunt, or spend time inside the operating room of an active combat hospital, or help the military mortician prepare the bodies to be sent home.

Common sense was no longer a factor in the plan of war by the time I arrived in Vietnam in 1969. Our capable military leaders were under complete control of the President and his selected click of miss-informed advisors. Military leaders trained and willing to either win the war or leave Vietnam had their hands tied by non-military idiots. Bomb or not to bomb extensively in North Vietnam was always up in the air. Control of targets was so idiotic it reached the level of recklessness. Helicopter pilots who came to visit our nurses told us of daily "Catch 22" experiences. Apparently targets had to be cleared with village Chiefs even if Viet Cong in black uniforms were seen crossing a bridge to or from the village. One helicopter pilot was reprimanded for firing on sappers emerging from the water onto a beach of a United States Military Rest and Recreation area. The pilot was told the target had to be cleared and he was not allowed to take the liberty of making a decision. Thank God he fired and saved the lives of American soldiers in the area.

Officers and enlisted men from the field were always telling horror stories associated with the "body count" concept. After each battle soldiers were sent out to count the number of American dead and the number enemy dead. The Army used the equation: American dead divided by enemy dead equals the body count ratio. A body count in our favor (we killed more than we lost) determined the success of the battle. Producing a high enemy body count and a low American body count was critical to promotion for many officers. Many generals established "production quotas" of battle based on body counts. A normal production rate might be killing ten enemy soldiers for each American soldier killed and a "highly skilled" unit was considered capable of killing fifty enemy for each dead American soldier. Some units actually had "Best of the Pack" contests between platoons based on body counts. The nightly news at home played up the body count when it was in our favor. Terrible stories were told of officers sending soldiers into unsafe "hot spots" to count the dead so an officer could enhance his chances of promotion. Little wonder 20% of American officers who died in Vietnam were assassinated by their own men. Soldiers told of body counts being inflated so the public would think we were winning the war. One of the ironies of the Vietnam War is: we lost over 58,800 and the enemy lost over 950,000. Who won? Body counts mean nothing; they only typify how moronic the war in Vietnam became.

Sources of information about what was happening in the United States, the Vietnam War, and the world were somewhat limited to those serving in Vietnam. In-country, the *Stars and Strips*, a military publication, was available, or you could listen to the Army radio station [*Good Morning-Vietnam*], or watch the military controlled TV. The military sources of information were severely sanitized for propaganda purposes; keep the troops uninformed and they will be more loyal, seemed to be the slogan. Those fortunate enough to be at a permanent base could look forward to out-of-date newspapers, magazines, and books from home. Our problem was not a lack of interest in current events but a lack of time to read and digest what was really happening.

Sometimes outright lies were detected. The Army television station re-broadcast news from the United States where the President said with great conviction: "We do not have troops in Cambodia and we will not have troops in Cambodia." After the broadcast I walked over to the operating room and asked the next ten soldiers to be operated on: "Where were you when you got shot?" Answers: all ten said Cambodia. Now who would you believe? Other deceits were not so easy to pick-up. Little wonder the soldiers in the field, isolated from information, became disenchanted about the war. Many developed a deep skepticism about what they were being told to justify the war. The GI slogan "it don't mean nothin'" became more popular as the war progressed.

Helicopters were not only recognized as life saving but as life giving to the soldiers. Supplies, replacements, and mail came to the firebase by helicopter; exiting the firebase were the dead, the wounded, outgoing mail and soldiers going home after completing one year in Vietnam. Helicopters were always in the air over Long Binh. We even had "crane" helicopters, used to lift items as large as a 2 ½ ton truck.

Waste, waste, waste. You never got used to the amount of trash a war generates. A sergeant on his third tour of duty told me that at the beginning of the war, if you needed a part for a broken down jeep it was much easier and faster to dig a hole, push the jeep in, cover it up, and report it as missing in action. Then you could request a new jeep and not have to wait for the part. A logistics officer took me to the Long Binh military dump. I saw piles of trucks, jeeps, helicopters, tanks, etc., stacked in cones about 50 to 60 feet high. The used equipment was sold as scrap metal to the Japanese for one cent on the dollar. By 1969, the supply line to Vietnam from the United States was well oiled. Nothing seemed to be lacking. Fresh fruit and vegetables, ice cream, and other food came to us daily from military farms in Thailand. Ammo, fuel, vehicles, helicopters, and other weapons of war were off loaded at a number of ports. When a firebase was closed, we walked away leaving everything behind for the enemy. Trash generated from the 24th Evacuation Hospital complex would fill a garbage dump as fast as any middle-sized town in the United States. When America pulled out of Vietnam, everything was left behind for the South Vietnamese, who were rapidly conquered by the NVA.

Waste was not just in material. What about the tremendous damage to the environment of Vietnam? Unknown numbers of animals were killed and crater holes from B-52 bombing raids pocked the landscape. The 58,000 names on the Vietnam War Memorial in Washington, D.C. will give you a vision of how many lives were wasted to fight a war without a moral cause. Touch the wall, feel the souls of those who died penetrate your hand as they tell you their love for America, then ask the poignant question: How much do you love America?

Names of wounded soldiers I treated have been completely lost to me. No effort on my part was made, except on a short-term basis, to remember the names of wounded soldiers. Intentional suppression? Perhaps. When I visit the Vietnam War Memorial it seems I always find myself reading the names from 1969 to 1970, hoping to recall just one name. Sometimes I remember the names of a few physicians or nurses but even that memory is vague unless associated with an event. Events, feelings, smells, etc., are imbedded to such an extent I feel I am still there reliving those days. Our minds must filter out information it deems unnecessary. A perplexing subject to say the least.

Zoe Leone Palmer, the girl I married. What effect did the Vietnam War have on our marriage? We grew up on the same street in a small town, attended the same schools, went to the same church, and even walked to school together once in a while. My dog used to scare Zoe Leone when she walked by my house. Our values, our hopes, our goals, our expectations, were all the same. Our foundation for marriage was built on solid ground with a commitment to stay together for eternity. Leaving Zoe Leone and four children was the hardest, heart-wrenching, act of my life. Tears poured down my cheeks on the plane to Alaska and then on to Vietnam. Many nights I just lay in bed thinking of her. Wonderful memories of marriage raced through my mind. Each of her daily letters was like a message to light up the dark spot I was living in. Words, wonderful words, of love, of events, of children growing up, of impressions, and of concern, elevated my soul for an instant out of the carnage I was knee deep in. Never did I question our love for each other. Was I tempted by the availability of other women? To look at, yes. To do anything physically, no. Man and wife are meant to serve out life, the good-the bad, together. Absence did not make the heart grow stronger. Absence made us grateful we had found each other before the war, had children, and were ready for whatever was required of us. Zoe Leone was of the same fiber I was made of. Our views of God, of America, and the Vietnam War were similar. The week of Rest and Recreation in Hawaii at mid-tour was a blessing. We went to the Hawaiian Temple and renewed our commitment to one another and to God the Father. What a spiritual experience to share after such a long separation. Our unity was a powerful factor in keeping me committed to my work and duty in Vietnam. Returning home to Zoe Leone and the children was the most positive event in my life after the Vietnam War.

The 24th Evacuation Hospital had a phenomenal record for trauma care. Less than 2% of wounded soldiers who arrived alive on the helicopter pad, died. American soldiers through out South Vietnam knew they had a 98% chance of survival if they could make it to an American hospital. No stateside hospital or combat hospital in previous wars have come close to this record. The downside of such a high survival rate was that soldiers now lived with injuries not compatible with life in previous wars. Many soldiers were sent home devoid of life's sensations and feelings. My job in Vietnam was to preserve life, within reason, and let the soldier and his family have the opportunity to shape a new life, sometimes good, sometimes bad. On the flip side, in the homes of many Veterans who would have not survived in previous wars, there are men leading productive lives. Who are we to make judgments on outcome? The medical and nursing professions require us to access the injury, repair the injury, and provide means for a reasonable recovery, both physically, and hopefully, spiritually.

Work was a saving grace for me in Vietnam. Sometimes I would be in the operating room for 36 to 48 hours at a time, with only short breaks for food and showers. Sleep came rapidly after intense work. Mass casualties were dependent on the actions of the enemy and our military plans. Occasionally three or four days would pass without a casualty. During these lulls we would spend the first twenty-four hours in bed sleeping or reading. Then the next few lull days would be filled with elective surgeries. Anything to keep boredom at bay. Listening to music, reading, studying, or talking to friends' filled idle time. Our mission in Vietnam was to take care of the wounded, a mission that kept me happy and sane. Fatigue helped to nullify the despair and loneliness of separation from home. Every day I tried to find time to write a letter or two. Mail call was the high point of any day. On occasion I went to the Long Binh telephone transmission station and made a call home. The connection was usually good but the place was so busy it was impossible to go on a regular basis.

Long Binh was the headquarters of the U.S. Army in South Vietnam and was the largest base in Vietnam. The size of the base and large numbers of soldiers allowed the Mormons to organize a small branch of the church. All the members were male. We met in an air-conditioned room at USARV headquarters. Two meetings were held every Sunday, priesthood and sacrament. My attendance was erratic because of casualty inflow. Church attendance was the highlight of the week for my spiritual being.

"Nation to Nation". "Friend to Friend". Trivial propaganda slogans heard every day. Our part in nation to nation and friend to friend was to send medical and dental teams to villages so the villagers would love Americans and hate the Viet Cong. It worked while we were in the village but when we left reality came slamming down on the villagers. The Viet Cong appeared and took fierce revenge, sometimes disemboweling the Village Chief for allowing Americans to visit the village.

France had tried to win over Indochina before us, had left, and told the United States not to get involved. Little did America know of the absolute determination of the North Vietnamese and Viet Cong. These men and women had the resolve to stick out the war despite how long it would take or the casualties required. Our leaders were always painting the enemy as weaklings. The enemy was resilient, tough, smart, courageous, and willing to sacrifice anything to re-unite Vietnam. North Vietnamese troops were well trained and recognized as one of the finest guerilla armies in the world. Contrast the enemy soldier with tire-treads for shoes, a packet of rice, a straw hat, and an AK-47 with the U.S. soldier carrying fifty pounds of "gear." Viet Cong were local villagers who saw the corrupt South Vietnamese government being supported by rich Americans. These men and women were determined to overthrow those in power in South Vietnam. America had no long-term commitment to the Vietnam War nor to South Vietnam. Americans did not understand the people or the place. Americans certainly underestimated the enemy. "Nation to Nation" and "Friend to Friend" was a failure in Vietnam.

The Vietnam War, from beginning to end, was an enormous deception by America's leaders. Truth was misrepresented for the sake of political expediency. Thomas Jefferson in 1785 said: *He who permits himself to tell a lie often finds it much easier to do it a second and third time, till at length it becomes habitual...* The United States was warned by the French, who had 500,000 troops in Indochina, not to get involved in a war between North and South Vietnam. The standing government in South Vietnam was corrupt, deceitful, and did not resemble in anyway a republic or democracy. America created a puppet state to glorify the "quest" to establish freedom in Vietnam. Efforts in Vietnam to stand against communism still remains unclear to me. General Westmoreland, the Commander of American forces in Vietnam, claimed the Vietnam War was the turning point for communism and was of great strategic importance to the free world. Many men and women who served in Vietnam and saw the disparity between what was said by America's leaders and what was happening in-country, came back disillusioned and, in some cases, angry. President Johnson in a speech 7 April 1965 said we were in Vietnam 1) *...because we have a promise to keep...,* 2) *...to strengthen world order,* 3) *...because there are great stakes in the balance,* and 4) *...in order to slow down aggression.* Noble, but non-specific, goals in 1965 as the war was beginning to escalate.

The majority of ordinary citizens in South Vietnam did not know the difference between communism and democracy. War had been their daily diet since birth. Could it be too much to ask to work without helicopters strafing the rice paddies or Viet Cong interrupting work by killings villagers and stealing the harvested rice? The only effective strategy for everyday Vietnamese survival was to side with whatever military force was present at any particular time, be it Viet Cong, American, French, North Vietnamese, or South Vietnamese. Vietnam was ravaged by the bombs of B-52s, the search and destroy missions of American troops, the napalm bombs of American fighter planes, and ruthless terrorism by the Viet Cong. Ordinary Vietnamese were trying to stay alive in a place so close to being hell that many welcomed death as a blessing.

I found it depressing to listen to the grunts tell of Colonels ordering platoon after platoon up a hill to "take it" on orders from a General and then marching away to leave the hill for the North Vietnamese. How could we glorify unimportant battles just to give the American public a false sense of the invincibility of American troops? Most stateside newspapers ran stories based on sanitized information from the daily briefing of the Army in Saigon. The relationship of such news to reality was about the same as riding through "It's a Small World" in Disneyland and thinking the entire world is peaceful and lovely!

Constant exposure to carnage makes you feel numb, unable to give or receive love, unable to feel or express happiness; nothing matters, so why exist? Many soldiers during and after the Vietnam war resorted to mind-altering substances, i.e. alcohol, street drugs, to escape reality. My exposure to continual carnage has been explained to me as being similar to the prolonged combat experienced by the grunts. The end result for me was a deadening of pain and desire, emotional coolness, and indifference. Development of new personal relationships or orally expressing love became extraordinarily difficult.

Leaders talk of a "limited war" was poppycock. At the peak of the war in 1969 there were over 550,000 soldiers stationed in Vietnam and thousands of others in Manila, Guam, and Thailand. Counting the number of people required for the logistic requirements of the Vietnam War, it would not be unreasonable to add a minimum of 100,000 the 550,000 figure. In 1969 it was estimated the combat capability of America in the Vietnam War had reached 40 per cent of all United States Army combat-ready divisions, more than 50 percent of Marine Corps divisions, 33 per cent of U.S. naval forces, and the U.S. Air Force had in use, 50 per cent of their fighter-bombers and 50 per cent of the B-52 bombers. How could this be labeled a "limited war"? The massive force of the U.S. dropped over 7,500,000 tons of bombs (three times the tonnage of WW II, an explosive force equal to 700 atomic bombs), 400,000 tons of napalm, 11,200,000 gallons of Agent Orange, 550 kilograms of deadly Dioxin, and used about 7,000,000 tons of munitions. We created over twenty-five million bomb craters in a country the size of California. It has been estimated the United States dropped over 1,000 pounds of explosive for every man, woman, and child in South Vietnam. This destructive force in Vietnam was many times that ever used in warfare. Yet a people whose per capita income in 1975 was estimated at $160 per year, defeated a country with a per capita income of over $6,000.

The cost in dollars spent for the Vietnam War is staggering. Estimates hover around a figure of $239 billion. By the end of the 1960s America was spending about $400,000 for every Viet Cong killed. The number of human lives lost has been estimated at:

American soldiers	58,800
South Korean soldiers	4,407
Australia and New Zealand soldiers	469
Thailand soldiers	351
South Vietnamese soldiers	220,000
North Vietnamese soldiers	440,000

There were over 300,000 U.S. soldiers wounded and about 150,000 of these wounded required hospitalization. Loss of money I can understand. Loss of human life and permanent disabilities are beyond comprehension. Was the battle worth the cost? Whatever your answer is I can assure you the Vietnam War cannot be considered a "limited war."

Many ask, why don't you just forget about the Vietnam War and get on with your life? Easy to say but hard to do. To forget about what happened in Vietnam would be a moral injustice for me. Forgetting the enemy may be possible, forgiving the despot leaders of America may be possible, but forgetting the dead and wounded is just not possible.

References:
1. Reporting Vietnam. Part one: American Journalism 1959-1969. Part two: American Journalism 1969-1975. The Library of America. Literary Classics of the United States, Inc., New York. N.Y. 1998

CHAPTER 10

AFTERMATH

RETURNING HOME IS HISTORICALLY SOMETHING soldiers have longed for and looked forward too. For me, returning home from the Vietnam War, in 1970, was a source of concern. Television depicted American soldiers being spit on in the San Francisco airport. Soldiers were mocked by Americans with derogatory statements like: *murderers, supporters of tyranny, child killers, depraved fiends, psychopathic killers*. What irony! American soldiers wore U. S. military uniforms on the plane from Vietnam but those who were not proceeding to out-processing at Oakland were instructed to change into civilian clothes in the San Francisco airport prior to boarding a connecting flight. No need to incite ridicule.

I arrived in my hometown of Cedar City, Utah in late summer of 1970, to pick up Zoe Leone and four children en route to a new assignment as Director of Anesthesia Research at Brooke Army Medical Center [BAMC] in San Antonio, Texas. In my youth our local Army National Guard unit upon returning from the Korean War had been honored as heroes with a big parade, a band and fine speeches. I was one of many returning singularly from the Vietnam War and received the same avoidance afforded those who came before me. People I had known all my life would greet me on the street with "How are you doing, I haven't seen you for a while. What have you been doing?" I would tell them I just got back from Vietnam. The next sentence would be something to the effect: "Well it is good to see you home. Isn't the weather great this time of year?" An immediate change of subject. A ruse to avoid discussion of a war they did not understand and did not care about. Even more heartbreaking was the reception received by my immediate family. My father and brother had missed serving in World War II and the Korean War. Neither understood what military commitment was except for the occasional Audie Murphy war movie on TV. My father asked how I was, was the war bad, and then cut off the conversation. No interest in what had gone on, what my impressions were of the war, nor any discussion of what the war was all about. My older brother didn't even ask a question about the war. I have never figured out if it was because he didn't care about the war, was afraid to discuss the war, was ashamed of my role in the war, or felt uncomfortable because he had never served in a war. Zoe Leone had received daily letters from Vietnam so she knew many of my feelings. Zoe Leone served as my leaning post, an outlet for the frustrations of the "welcome" in our hometown.

When I came home, I desperately wanted to talk to someone about the blood bath I had participated in in Vietnam. Blood on our clothes, blood on our boots, blood on the floor, and blood on the wounded soldiers. Constantly viewing grossly disfigured human bodies, still alive, from the battlefield. All young men, average age 23, dedicated, idealistic, wet behind the ears, patriotic, naive to the realities of war, fearful, and yet willing to fight for what was called the preservation of freedom. Young men crying and begging to let them die rather than have to face their sweethearts without a leg, an arm, a penis, or a severely disabling facial wound. Men who revered our help in saving their life but knew the limitations in our ability to restore what had been blown away.

Repeated, repeated, repeated, days and nights bathed in blood and buried in piles of amputated arms and legs. Repeated, repeated, repeated scenarios of blown out eye orbits, gunshot wounds of the head leaving gaping holes in the skull and permanently comatose soldiers, acrid smells from intestines full of holes hanging out of gaping wounds in the abdomen, urine flowing from holes and gashes in the urinary bladder, and gross disfiguration of faces caused by gunshot and mine wounds. Contending daily with dirt and grim, sometimes including maggots, in the wounds of American soldiers. Having enemy soldiers, 14-16 years old, spit in your face as you attempted to render them anesthesia care.

Returning to BAMC was a relief. Familiar surroundings and military personnel could sympathize with the feelings in my heart. I had returned to hospital beds filled with injured soldiers from Vietnam who were now undergoing reconstructive surgery and physical therapy. Men confined to wheelchairs or Striker frames for life. Many times on the ward your heart was ripped out as deformed soldiers cried out, not about their injuries, but about the terrible attitudes of their family and other Americans about the Vietnam War. Was it a disgrace to lose arms, legs, etc., for your country? If not, why were citizens of the country that drafted you and ordered you to serve in the Vietnam War calling you a "murderer?"

Helicopters evacuating casualties flew nearly 500,000 missions, bringing 900,000 soldiers (half of them Americans) to U.S. military hospitals in Vietnam. *"The Wall"* in Washington, D. C. has 58,169 names engraved. Over 2,590,000 American served in the Vietnam War. Amputations and crippling wounds were 300 per cent higher than in World War II. Today it is estimated over 75,000 Vietnam veterans are disabled.

My mind closed slowly to the citizen betrayals and excuses of politicians who did not lose a son or daughter in the Vietnam War. My solace was found within the military community among people who identified with my plight. In hindsight, I defensively withdrew into a protective shell, suppressed intense feelings, and became a workaholic to avoid thinking about what I had seen and done. I am grateful for having the opportunity to provide the best trauma care in the world to the soldiers in Vietnam.

Life went on. The war ended about a year before I completed my payback time for training. I toyed with the idea of staying in the Army for a career but decided against it because changes of assignment were common and I wanted to be a part of an anesthesia teaching program. I left the Army in 1973 and entered the civilian sector.

In 1975, I entered anesthesia private practice in a small town in Southern Utah. Here I was to stay for six years. During many hours giving anesthesia it emerged I had been in the military and served in Vietnam. Responses were mixed; some interested, some disinterested. Only one young physician became a heckler. Apparently he was eligible for the draft when he finished his residency training and had contacted the local draft board to see what was necessary for a healthy physician to get an exemption from the draft. According to his story, a small town can request an exemption if the need for the physician is absolutely desperate and vital to the medical care of the community. Since he grew up in this small Southern Utah town he was able to convince the local draft board to grant him an exemption from the draft. He stayed with his family in the quiet luxury of a peaceful town while his classmates served in the military, many in Vietnam. Upon my arrival he repeatedly reminded me of how stupid the Vietnam War had been, how smart and clever he was to have "pulled the right strings" to avoid the draft, and what an idiot I had been to serve in the Vietnam War. Today, as I look back, I realize he was only trying to justify his lack of patriotism and responsibility and hide his cowardice. Many physicians are egotistical, placing themselves above the common man, and justify such arrogance by the slippery statement "I am a physician, therefore, I am better than you." Physicians with such an attitude deserve no respect or recognition. Physicians should spurn conceit and be grateful for the opportunity to learn a subject as fascinating as medicine and to serve their fellow men.

It was not until 1985 that I decided to re-join the reserve component of the Army. I served two years in the Army 144th Evacuation Hospital, Utah National Guard, in Salt Lake City as a reserve officer before I accepted a job in Ohio. I transferred to the Navy reserve in 1988 because 1] my son was in the Navy, 2] I did not like the hospital tents with dirt floors in the Army, and 3] I wanted to do my two summer training and weekend drills at the military medical school, the Uniformed Services University of Health Sciences [USUHS] in Bethesda, Maryland. In late August, 1990 I was called to active duty for *Desert Shield* [renamed *Desert Storm* when the shooting started]. I was given 48 hours to get things in order and report to the National Naval Medical Center [NNMC] in Bethesda, MD. The staff of the NNMC was on board the hospital ship *Comfort* steaming to the Persian Gulf when the reservists arrived at the hospital. Being back on active duty was a real treat and I enjoyed the twelve months at NNMC. At the close of *Desert Storm,* the Navy offered me the opportunity to stay on active duty; I declined and went into private practice in Salt Lake City, Utah.

During two years of private practice in Salt Lake City, Utah, I stayed in the U.S. Navy Reserve. Working 14-16 hours every day with night call twice a week was not very appealing. Two or three times I attempted to cut down my hours but the anesthesia group did not want to hire any more anesthesiologists because it would mean less money in their pockets. Time for family, church, and self were more important to me so I decided to go back on active duty. The Navy had their "quota" filled for anesthesiologists at the time but I was fortunate enough to know the right people and was allowed to join because of my academic record. My requested assignment to the Department of Anesthesiology at USUHS was granted. A great job, working with medical students and interacting with anesthesia residents doing research projects at the school. One or two of the military faculty had served in Vietnam and it was refreshing to talk to someone who had similar thoughts. On one occasion I needed some slides of wounded soldiers for a lecture and was referred to an obscure office in the basement of the Walter Reed Institute of Research. Inside the office was archived the injuries of the dead soldiers of the Vietnam War. Cabinets and cabinets full of pictures organized by the type of injury causing death. A gruesome place to visit. Someone was using the data to document the number and type of fatal injuries, weaponry patterns causing deaths, and, hopefully, determine how to better protect soldiers from death.

The Chairman position in the Department of Anesthesiology at Madigan Army Medical Center [MAMC] in Ft. Lewis, Washington, became available in 1994. An extensive internal search by the Army was unsuccessful in finding the kind of leader the Commanding General wanted. The Army turned to the Air Force and Navy for candidates. My name emerged as a candidate. At the time I was being considered for a similar leadership position at Naval Hospital, San Diego. An Admiral from the Office of the Surgeon General of the Navy called to "encourage" me to accept the position at MAMC. After a through discussion with the family and other Navy physicians, we accepted the position. As Chairman of the Department of Anesthesia and Operative Service, at what I considered to be the best hospital in the military, I was a very busy man.

After three years at MAMC, my twenty years of military service in the Army-Navy Reserve was completed. We made the decision to retire just before my 60th birthday [You must be 60 years old to receive retirement pay from the military reserve].

One night, a few months before leaving active duty, I was lying down to go to bed when I was overcome with a distinct feeling of imminent death. A rapid heart rate combined with hyperventilation led to the self-diagnosis of severe anxiety. I was frightened because I had never had symptoms like these before. My wife did not know what to do except hold me during the fifteen-minute episode. Intermittent nightly episodes began occurring, some lasting minutes, others hours; I was constantly looking for a medical reason to explain what was happening to me. Nighttime was faced with fear and trepidation, wondering if an anxiety attack would occur. For the first time in my life there was something I could not control; loss of control for someone like me is a disaster. As luck or destiny would have it, I was scheduled for a Navy course for those mustering out. A counselor from the Veterans Administration discussed the Vietnam War Post-Traumatic Stress Disorder [PTSD]. His slide of symptoms was almost a carbon copy of my symptoms. How could I, a physician, never in the jungle, suffer from PTSD? I called, made an appointment, and found out the anxiety attacks were the way my brain was releasing pent up emotions of the Vietnam War. It was not necessary to be in the jungle to get PTSD; constant exposure to death, carnage, blood, pain, crying, misery, and helplessness was all it took. My mind had been a kettle of water on low heat that had finally come to the boiling point and was now letting off steam. Thoughts of separation from the military had triggered the anxiety attacks. Repeated anxiety attacks were only the steam, the kettle was still on boil and full of water to be released. The counselor, David Holden, became my friend as we visited weekly and I poured out my feelings. David had served in Vietnam and was counseling a number of Veterans with PTSD. After a number of visits, I came to realize that PTSD was the root cause of my anger, depression, thoughts of suicide, lack of trust in anyone except Zoe Leone, and growing cynicism and skepticism.

PTSD triggered by war has not been limited to the Vietnam War. Out of World War I came the concept that exploding artillery shells caused actual physiological damage to the nervous system, hence, "shell shock." Psychiatric casualties suffering from the symptoms of "shell shock" were not uncommon in World War II and the Korean War. The term "shell shock" was eventually changed to "combat stress" and during the Vietnam War evolved to Post-Traumatic Stress Disorder. PTSD was much more common in the Vietnam War than in WWII or the Korean War. The average infantryman in World War II saw about 40 days of actual combat in four years. In the Vietnam War, the average infantryman had 240 days of combat in one year. During the Vietnam War, planes picked up a soldier in the United States and 24 hours later a helicopter dropped him in a jungle in Vietnam. When the soldier was scheduled to leave Vietnam, a helicopter lifted him out of the jungle floor and 24 hours later he off-loaded from a plane in his hometown. No time was allowed for talking with other soldiers to ease the pain of war. No time to sit on board a slow moving ship and exchange horror stories of the war with other soldiers bound for home. No time to defuse the atrocious experiences of war; experiences now to be bottled up until death. Vietnam veterans have a high rate of homelessness and suicide. Many veterans do not know that symptoms and changes in their lives are due to PTSD. Being in the medical field did not exclude me from ignorance of my own disorder.

My depression seemed to come and go in intermittent cycles. At one time I thought I might be manic-depressive but the symptoms did not fit the diagnosis. Despite positions of leadership and praise, I had continual feelings of worthlessness, which was a total mystery to Zoe Leone. My peers seemed to be isolated and distant from me. I did not have the tolerance to talk things through. More and more I wanted to be alone in my office or home engrossed in writing a paper or devising new ideas for the department. Sometimes I day-dreamed living the life of a hermit get away from all the stresses, be with nature, and have time to contemplate the real meaning of life. I would sometimes withdraw from everything as a method of coping. Crowds did, and still do, make me very uncomfortable. Going to an event in an open stadium was much less stressful than a crowded movie theater. A crowd triggers a closed in feeling that wraps around me and I attempt to break the invisible bond and flee. Only my intense love of music and plays motivates me enough to be able to tolerate a two or three-hour session with collected humanity.

Since the Vietnam War, our extended family has dubbed me the "wandering gypsy." After living in one place for a period of time, restlessness sets in. As an academic anesthesiologist with private practice experience, it is not hard to find a good job. One element of PTSD is to search for a safe place, a haven from problems. When we moved from one town to another it was my policy to make a clean break. No contacts with past acquaintances except for professional necessities. Criss-crossing the continent was one way to isolate myself from others.

Unexplained anger crept into my life. Some days I wake up angry, un-talkative, and leave the house as soon as possible, to avoid venting the anger on the family. Search for a reason or trigger for the anger has been fruitless and frustrating. No special circumstance seems to precede the emotion of anger. Once I was at a mall and had purchased food. I looked for a place to sit down, found an empty chair, and was told it was "saved" for someone else. I was very angry. My reaction to the situation was inappropriate and bothered me for a long time. Working long hours was the only way I could keep my mind off the Vietnam War. My anger has never been associated with physical outbursts. Verbal expressions with a stern tone of voice were infrequent but did occur to the dismay of the family.

Love is one positive emotion I have kept locked up inside since childhood. The Vietnam War just put a bigger padlock in place. Two notable exceptions have penetrated my barrier: love for Zoe Leone and love for my Father in Heaven. Mom and Dad did not have a loving relationship. Not once in my life did I see Dad kiss Mom, put his arm around her, or speak to her in a loving way. I grew up believing the "macho man" did not express love because it was a sign of weakness. Experiences in Vietnam served to verify that expressing love was not manly. Only through continual diligence have I learned to give love to our children and two or three friends. Over the years my persistent effort to express love has broken down some barriers with my seven children. Recently a flood of emotions, held inward for thirty years, has begun to emerge. Often I find myself tearful as I examine a beautiful flower, hear a touching story, see a sad movie, or read beautiful words expressed in books or scriptures. Emotions are emerging, sometimes untethered. It is as though the water in the kettle is flowing down the open hillside.

Surfacing of pent emotions is frightening, especially for someone who feels they must be in control or they are weak. I was afraid that if I allowed myself to feel emotional I might not stop crying. Following the Vietnam War, I began to slowly lose the capacity to love and care for others. Rendering care to a civilian trauma victim instantly brought back forceful, unpleasant memories of the Vietnam War. One enigma for me has been the ability to willingly help the disabled in the hospital setting but avoid them in the public setting. Throughout the ordeal I have been blessed to have maintained a purpose in life and know the reason for my existence on earth.

Since the Vietnam War, events important to others have not had the same impact on me. My wife often found it distressing that I would be rather unresponsive to my children's illnesses. Death boiled down to the philosophy "If you die, you die." Not an attitude to endear one to others. Little tolerance or patience is shown towards those who moan about a lack of material things. Mansion size homes, big cars, expensive clothes, are just not high on my priority list. Seeing people viciously pursuing money and alienating their loved ones is distressing. Those who consciously and willingly self-mutilate their body with tattoos, rings in all places, and adorn their bodies with expensive jewelry and changing fashions, seems superficial, vain, and lacking in intelligence.

Replicas of the Vietnam War have played an important part in healing my emotional wounds. The first time I touched "The Wall" at the Vietnam War Memorial in Washington, D.C. released a flood of emotions. Every time I visit Washington, D.C., I stop for at least a moment at "The Wall." Each time tears run down my cheeks. The life size Three Service Men statue at the *Vietnam War Memorial* serves to remind me of the reality of war. Little wonder I bought a book about "The Wall", a large picture of a Veteran touching "The Wall" with shadows of his dead buddies touching him, and a small replica of the *Three Service Men* statue for my office. Replicas and symbols have provided a source of spiritual healing.

Over the years the movie industry has made feeble attempts to depict the Vietnam War; just as they did with films like *Sergeant York* for World War I, and *To Hell and Back,* the autobiography of Audie Murphy, the most decorated combat soldier of World War II. One of the best depictions of medical care in combat was the series *Mash* based on the Korean War. Over the years I have found myself drawn to war movies, especially the Vietnam War. Examples of my favorites are *Good Morning Vietnam, Platoon,* and *Hanoi Hilton.* War cannot be depicted on the screen. *Saving Private Ryan,* of recent vintage, was well done as was *Platoon* and *Hanoi Hilton.* It is difficult to create a story line throughout a war movie. War is chaotic, unpredictable, and impossible to recreate. Our best actors cannot display the gut-wrenching fear, white knuckles, dry mouth, and multiple triggered autonomic nervous system defense mechanisms a combat soldier on jungle patrol experiences.

You cannot, and would not want to, fill the movie theater with the smells, environmental conditions, and carnage associated with real war. Best to stop wars, but, as General Patton said, "God, I love it"; men relish the cry to battle.

Healing of emotional wounds is not as rapid as healing of physical wounds, nor as observable. I only wish I could debride my emotional wounds and suture them up, but this is only a pipedream. I continue to be in on a roller coaster; some days up, some days down. However, I have noticed the ups and downs are not so far apart in height, encouraging me to hope the hills and valleys may someday be only ripples on an open plain. Each day is now faced with the view of eternity. Individual challenges are now looked back on as "what does this really mean in the perspective of eternity? Will this event that triggered anger really mean anything a day, a month, or a year from now? Perspective without analysis and control, have helped me to understand and accept the emotional outpouring from the Vietnam War. Spiritually has been strengthened by my persistent effort to draw closer to God the Father. Only He can look inside, understand, and help me serve my family and fellowmen.

In July, 1993, a reunion of all those who served in the 24th Evacuation Hospital from 1966 to 1972 was held in Washington, D.C. I did not attend. One letter from a former wounded soldier treated at the hospital was included in the pre-registration material for the reunion. His name was not included in the letter so permission to publish the letter in his words was not obtainable. I will have to paraphrase some of his remarks in hopes you, the reader, will feel his gratitude for the care he received at the 24th Evacuation Hospital. This average soldier, as he referred to himself, did not know who his caregivers were so he referred to them as the people of the 24th Evacuation Hospital. He made it clear he was writing not only for himself but for the hundreds who had been treated at the 24th Evacuation Hospital during the Viet Nam war years. He recalls arriving at the hospital and described how he was taken care of by various members of the staff, including the chaplain and the Red Cross attaché. I was touched by the fact he felt he was being treated by professionals who wanted him to be healed. He pulled my heart strings when he thanked us for being alive and told us he would remember us always.

Perhaps the best summary statement for this book would be the remarks I expressed at my retirement ceremony at MAMC:

Two score and ten years ago a scrawny, young, boy, age 9, played Army in the foxhole he dug in the backyard. He fought enemies without faces but with names: Hitler, Mussolini, and Tojo. Eight years later, when a senior in high school, he joined and became a private in Battery B, Artillery, Utah National Guard. Since then I have associated with the U.S. Army or U.S. Navy, either on active duty or in some kind of reserve status.

Why the military? Most likely it was the result of the patriotism instilled in me through our educational system, the Boy Scouts of America, and my Church. My values and beliefs were further catalyzed by my love and deep admiration of two of our nation's Founding Fathers: George Washington and Thomas Jefferson.

Where did I look for the bastion of the core values of America? To me the military did, does, and will remain the bastion for the elements of freedom. **Duty, Honor, Country,** the legend on the West Point Coat of Arms, reverently dictates what each citizen should do, what they can do, and what they must do to preserve our precious liberty.

When I went to Vietnam as a young anesthesiologist, I learned a number of lessons:

Lesson: Patriotism is not a fear of something, it is a love of something.

Lesson: Observing the continual 24-hour carnage in the operating room of the 24th Evacuation Hospital affirmed to me the truism: War is HELL!! Why? Because men lose their morals, they lose their spirit, and they lose their lives.

Lesson: The family we leave behind makes the greatest sacrifice. Zoe Leone continued to struggle with the raising of four children under the age of six without my daily input and support.

Lesson: Plato was right: **Only the dead have seen the end of war.**

My professional and military careers have been exceptionally full of diversity, challenge, and, most of all, fun. Following each avenue of opportunity has allowed me to fulfill an early life goal: Maintain a balanced life.

I firmly believe the United States of America is the "home of the brave" and the "land of the free." Our Father in Heaven protected the soil we walk on in this land for centuries, awaiting the arrival of men and women destined to establish again a democracy.

My desire has always been to serve my country, my family, and my God. May the flag of the United States always remind the world that men and women have the freedom to choose. I do hope some of my words have renewed the glimmer of fire in your eyes for the descriptive terms representing the United States of America: Liberty, Freedom, Democracy.

References:
Goodwin J: The etiology of combat-related post-traumatic stress disorders. Disabled American Veterans. National Headquarters. P.O. Box 14301. Cincinnati, OH 45214

PUBLICATIONS FROM MY VIETNAM EXPERIENCE

1. Petty WC, Mendenhall MK: A practical approach to anesthetic management in severe trauma. Journal American Association Nurse Anesthetists 1973;41:53-56
2. Kesler MG, Petty WC: Massive blood transfusion and resuscitation in the severely injured patient. Journal American Association Nurse Anesthetist 1971;39:105-118
3. Anesthesia, resuscitation and early care of wounded, use of morphine. Department of Army Technical Bulletin TB MED 234, Ago3143A, pp. 1-6, 1971
4. Fleming WH, Bowen JC, Petty C: The use of pulmonary compliance as a guide to respirator therapy. Surgery, Gynecology, Obstetrics 1972;134:291-292
5. Petty WC, Fleming WH: A simple technic for measuring lung compliance. Anesthesia Analgesia 1971;50:546-547
6. Petty C, Taylor W: Inhalation therapy: Experience in an Army Evacuation Hospital in Vietnam. Military Medicine 1971;136:891-893
7. Fleming WH, Petty C, Gielchinsky I: Evolution of an intensive care unit in Vietnam. American Surgeon 1973;39:422-423
8. Gielchinsky I, Petty C, Dierdorff S: Treatment of hemorrhagic necrosis within a pheochromocytoma with symptoms of acute abdomen. American Surgeon 1972;38:380-384
9. Kapp JP, Gielchinsky I, Petty C, McClure C: An internal shunt for use in the reconstruction of dural venous sinuses. Journal Neurosurgery 1971;35:351-354

ABBREVIATIONS, EPONYMS, AND DEFINITIONS

Agent Orange – A toxic defoliating agent dropped on the jungles of South Vietnam

AK-47 – The automatic weapon commonly used by the enemy

Article 15 – A law applied to military personnel in the military system of jurisprudence

ARVN – Army of the Republic of Vietnam (South Vietnam Army)

BAMC – Brooke Army Medical Center. Army hospital in Ft. Sam Houston, Texas

Catch 22 – A term that has come to mean a situation that is made worse no matter what you do, good or bad

Conghoa General Hospital – South Vietnamese Army hospital in Saigon, South Vietnam

CRNA – Certified Registered Nurse Anesthetist

Dioxin – Each of three unsaturated cyclic compounds or a derivative of such a compound

ECG – Electrocardiogram. Machine for monitoring the heart

Firebase – An area cut out of the jungle, leveled and defended as an outpost by the military

Grunt – American soldier fighting in the jungle

Hanoi Hilton – The prisoner of war compound in downtown Hanoi, North Vietnam. Affectionately called the "Hanoi Hilton" by its' American inmates

Hickam AFB – A United States Air Force base in Honolulu, Hawaii

Hooch – Where we slept

ICU – Intensive care unit

IPPB – Intermittent positive pressure breathing. Respiratory therapy used in lung disease

Kick Bucket – The garbage can in the operating room with wheels so it could be easily moved by a kick

Long Binh – U. S. Army post near Saigon, South Vietnam. Largest military base in Vietnam

M-16 – The automatic weapon commonly used by American soldiers

MACV – Military Assistance Command Vietnam. Headquarters commanding the American Forces in South Vietnam, 1962-1973

Mamason – Female Vietnamese civilians hired to clean our hooch's

MAMC – Madigan Army Medical Center. Army hospital in Ft. Lewis, Washington

MATS – Military Air Transport service

MedEvac – Medical evacuation. Usually applied to helicopter evacuating wounded soldiers to hospitals

MP – Military police

MPC – Military payment certificates. Issued in place of American dollars for currency. Used by United States troops in South Vietnam

MSC – Medical Service Corp Officer

Napalm – A thixotropic gel consisting of petrol and a thickening agent. Used in flame throwers and incendiary bombs. Jellied petrol

Ncocmon – A strongly fermented fish sauce

NNMC – National Naval Medical Center. Navy hospital in Bethesda, MD

NVA – North Vietnamese Army. The Army of North Vietnam

Oath of Hippocrates – An oath written by the Father of Medicine, Hippocrates, and taken by some American Physicians to indicate their devotion to the ethical and moral foundations of medicine

OJT – On-the-job training. Learning skills on the job while under the supervision of someone

POW – Prisoner of War

PTSD – Post Traumatic Stress Disorder

PX – Post Exchange

R & R – Rest and recreation

Rube Goldberg – Making do with what you have at hand. i.e. fixing a broken object with "duct tape" and airplane glue

Saigon – The capital city of South Vietnam. Renamed by the communists Ho Chi Minh City

Sapper – Viet Cong dressed in black that infiltrated at night on search and destroy missions

TAMC – Tripler Army Medical Center. Army hospital in Honolulu, Hawaii

Tan Son Nhut AFB – USAF base just outside Saigon, south Vietnam

TET – A national holiday celebrated in South Vietnam

The Wall – A Memorial on the grounds of the Washington, D.C. mall with the names of the soldiers killed in the Vietnam War.

USARV – United States Army Republic Vietnam

USUHS – Uniformed Services University of the Health Sciences. The U.S. military medical school in Bethesda, Maryland

VA – Veterans Administration

Viet Cong – South Vietnamese who were determined to overthrow the South Vietnam government

WRAIR – Walter Reed Institute of Research. Army medical research center in Washington, D.C.

Printed in the United States
By Bookmasters